# Poetry of the People

# Poetry of the People:
## Poems to the President, 1929–1945

## Donald W. Whisenhunt

**Bowling Green State University Popular Press**
**Bowling Green, OH 43403**

Library of Congress Cataloging-in-Publication Data
Whisenhunt, Donald W.
    Poetry of the people  :  poems to the president, 1929-1945 /
Donald W. Whisenhunt.
        p.    cm.
    Includes bibliographical references and index.
    ISBN 0-87972-703-9. -- ISBN 0-87972-704-7 (pbk.)
    1. American poetry--20th century--History and criticism.
2. Politics and literature--United States--History--20th century.
3. Popular literature--United States--History and criticism. 4. Political
poetry, American--History and criticism.  5. Presidents--United
States--Poetry.  6. American poetry--20th century.  7. Political poetry,
American.  I. Title.
PS310.P6W48   1996
811'.5208--dc20                                                    96-20028
                                                                        CIP

Cover design by Gary Dumm

# Contents

*For Alexandra and Meredith*

*What It's All About*

# Preface

I first became aware of the large collection of poetry in the Franklin D. Roosevelt Library more than thirty years ago. While there researching for my doctoral dissertation, I began to see the occasional poem scattered through the various collections. When I inquired of the staff, I was told there were forty boxes of poetry and forty boxes of music in separate collections.

My doctoral advisor, Timothy P. Donovan, suggested that there might be some research opportunities there, but he strongly urged me to complete the dissertation and not get distracted by this material, since it was not central to my work at the time. He was correct. I put the poems aside, vowing to get back to them soon.

In the late 1960s I published an article based on them in an early issue of the *Journal of Popular Culture*. Then I became interested in other projects, and the poetry was laid aside again. For the next twenty-five years or so, my career took a different direction. During that time, my thoughts continued to go back to the poetry, and from time to time I dipped into the material.

In 1991 I left academic administration and went back to my first love, the classroom and the library. At that time I resolved to complete a book on the people's poetry that had been haunting me for so many years. This is finally the culmination of that project.

I have incurred many debts over the years in this long-running project. The staffs at both the Roosevelt Library and the Hoover Library were invaluable in helping me locate the poetry and in making copies for me. Several times over the years I went back to them, either in person or by mail, and despite changes in staff, I was always treated with the utmost professionalism.

I have also had support in the form of small travel grants and small grants for obtaining material from Thiel College, Eastern New Mexico University, and the University of Texas at Tyler. I would like to acknowledge and thank those institutions at this time.

My two sons, Donald and Ben, grew to adulthood hearing about the depression poetry. They didn't know much about what I did when they were young, but as they grew up they encouraged me to continue with the project. Now they are adults and have children of their own. It is only fitting that I dedicate this to those two new grand-daughters.

My wife, Betsy, has always been supportive of my professional career. She recognized early that the poetry collection was a gold mine that I should develop. She has been especially encouraging in this project since I returned to teaching full-time. Her support has always meant very much to me.

I am pleased that this labor of love is finally coming to fruition. I think the people's poetry says much about America in the 1930s and I hope that I have been able to convey much of that in these pages. All errors of fact and interpretation, of course, are mine.

Donald W. Whisenhunt
Bellingham, Washington
January 1996

# 1

# Introduction

Americans, from their earliest beginnings, have been a politically motivated people. Even though the earliest governments in the colonies might not have been very democratic, they were much more advanced than anywhere else in the world. Basic to the concept of democracy or representative government, no matter how restricted, is communication between governors and the governed. From the very early period in the American colonies even average citizens felt they could influence the affairs of state by communication, either verbal or written, with the officials who represented them. As the American system of federalism and the emphasis on local government developed more strongly, average citizens became more jealous of their right to communicate with those in power.

Formal and informal studies have shown that public officials in all periods have been the target of those citizens with opinions and something to say. The most common form of communication usually is letter-writing. After the development of the telegraph, this form of communication was used widely, especially if citizens wished to inform their representatives quickly. Later the telephone offered more rapid communication, but for average citizens its use has been somewhat restricted due to cost and because telephone calls are easier to forget than written messages. For the historian telephone communication is obviously less valuable since records are not always kept, but even when they are, they do not record the language of the caller. Thus, letters and telegrams continue to be a major source for the historian to learn about communication between citizens and their government.

On virtually all occasions the citizen has been quick to inform public officials when they have been wise, stupid, or uninformed on public issues. The letter writer has little hesitation in advising public officials on the most sensitive and complicated public matters and in being incensed when that advice is not taken. Some of the most audacious suggestions imaginable have been made, and often the language is so abusive that it could not be used in polite society.

An example of the passions that can be aroused can be found in any period of crisis. John F. Kennedy told of several examples of constituent pressure on Senators and how they reacted. Seldom do public figures tell their constituents their true feelings. One exception came from Congressman John Steven McGroarty in 1934 and bears quoting.

> One of the countless drawbacks of being in Congress is that I am compelled to receive impertinent letters from a jackass like you in which you say I promised to have the Sierra Madre mountains reforested and I have been in Congress two months and haven't done it. Will you please take two running jumps and go to hell.[1]

Many times letters and responses were not so abusive; instead they were little short of amazing. Average citizens often think they have solutions to major problems that are ignored because they are not in positions of power. Occasionally, a leader comes along who arouses such confidence and admiration that average citizens believe he will be receptive to their ideas. One such man was Franklin D. Roosevelt.

After his election but before the inauguration, while he was putting his cabinet together and formulating plans to be followed after he was in power, numerous people tried to influence the actions he would take. Two examples will suffice to show the confidence the public had in FDR and the belief that he was open to new ideas. Such examples also reveal something of the nature of the letter writer.

One letter received by Roosevelt from a Texan promised to end the depression if only Roosevelt would help him.

> In all it will take me 120 days to put every single individual to work. I have an editor whom I prefer to be my secretary and you must give me this preference. I need 5 reporters and 5 secret service men for a body guard. I need an assistant secretary whom you may choose. I also need 2 stenographers and 2 messengers. Traveling expenses to be paid by the government. My salary will be $25,000 a year and expenses for a term of four years.[2]

This correspondent never revealed the specifics of how he would accomplish this feat. Someone on Roosevelt's staff was so amazed by this letter that the following notation was made: "The 8th wonder of the world."[3]

Another example was the newspaper editor from eastern New Mexico who had devised a new economic system. He was convinced that Roosevelt would accept it as a solution to the world's problems if he only knew more about it. Therefore, he wrote Roosevelt asking for a personal appointment in January ("while milking is light—we operate a dairy ranch as well as a newspaper"). He said he believed the matter to be of such importance that he would undertake the personal expense necessary to visit FDR. He also promised total secrecy to protect the president-elect as well as himself until they were able to agree and announce their joint plans to the public.[4] The reply from Roosevelt's secretary pleaded a full schedule and invited him to write again if he wished.[5] Despite the fact that the responses from public officials may have been discourteous or noncommittal, most people continued to write to express their opinions.

Studies have shown that political letter-writing peaked during times of crisis. The Civil War was perhaps the first in which the volume of mail shot up to massive proportions. An analysis of Lincoln's mail revealed that he received letters praising his efforts to maintain the Union, letters from Northerners attacking his policies as leading to war, and letters from unhappy Southerners who saw him as the incarnation of evil. Other major crises such as the Spanish-American War and World War I were so important that one would expect the volume of mail to rise. Domestic crises too raised the volume of political letters. The impeachment of Andrew Johnson brought intense pressure on the members of the Senate who had to judge the president.

In all these earlier periods the volume of mail would swell during a crisis and then settle back to a more normal level during periods of calm. The intensity of public feeling during a turbulent period can be more easily studied by analyzing the mail of public officials, especially the president. Probably one could chart or graph the political history of the United States by the rise and fall in the volume of mail.

Mail continued to fluctuate in quantity until the 1930s when a permanent change in political letter-writing can be seen. The Great Depression was, by any definition, a crisis of major proportions. Not only did the economic system so highly praised and revered for generations utterly fail to meet the challenge, but the social fabric was strained as it had never been before. In this situation the volume of presidential mail soared far beyond what it had ever been. In addition, the decade of the 1930s became a period of transition when mass political letter-writing became established. When the depression came to an end the volume of mail did not decrease. In truth political letter-writing passed beyond the stage of a crisis phenomenon and became a permanent part of the political scene.[6]

Some have suggested that this change was due to the character and personality of Franklin Roosevelt. As already mentioned, the public seemed more at ease with him than they had with any president for some time. Certainly the two most recent presidents—Hoover and Coolidge—

were not the warm and open type of men who encouraged public adoration and sympathy. They had many admirers and supporters, but it was difficult for the public to feel close to them. Roosevelt, on the other hand, was the kind of person who attracted people and made them feel as though they were old friends even if they had never met. The informal and personal nature of many of the letters received by FDR reflect this feeling from the public.

Communications received by Roosevelt were of various kinds. All presidents had received letters but his surpassed all records. The letters he received were of the most praiseworthy and the most condemnatory. Few presidents raised the passion that he did. Some would argue that there were only two emotions or feelings among the American people about this most unusual man: love and hate. Clearly the personality of the president was a major factor in the increase in political mail received at the White House.

At least five excellent books are available on political letter-writing in general and on the depression and Roosevelt in particular. Ira Smith[7] was the Chief of Mails at the White House for about fifty years. He became a clerk there in 1897 and gradually assumed responsibility for all incoming mail. In a breezy informal way, Smith traces the development of a system for handling the mail as the volume grew to larger and larger proportions. In discussing this one facet of presidential operations, Smith gives an informative and often amusing account of the growth of the presidency into a complex bureaucratic operation.

Leila Sussmann[8] made a thorough study of the mail received by Roosevelt. Anyone who has worked at the Roosevelt Library in the attractive community of Hyde Park, New York, knows how massive a task it is to analyze the thousands (or even millions) of pieces of mail that went to Roosevelt. Despite the handicaps, Sussmann provides us with a good overall view of what political letter-writing became in the 1930s.

The third study is *All But the People: Franklin D. Roosevelt and His Critics, 1933-39* by George Wolfskill and John A. Hudson.[9] In this very helpful and valuable work most of the emphasis was on the criticism that Franklin Roosevelt received as president. The thesis here is that it seemed that everyone hated Roosevelt if the papers and the letters are to be believed. Everyone seemed to hate him except for the people who elected him to four unprecedented terms as president. Wolfskill and Hudson not only used the extensive materials in the Roosevelt Library but they relied heavily upon other collections, especially the Valentine Collection at the University of Texas at Austin "which probably includes more anti-Roosevelt material than any collection extant."[10]

The fourth book to use these resources is *Down and Out in the Great Depression*, edited by Robert S. McElvaine.[11] In this excellent work McElvaine quotes extensively from letters written by average persons during the depression. He concentrates almost entirely on letters and does not include much poetry.

The fifth is a book done in the 1980s called *"Slaves of the Depression": Workers' Letters About Life on the Job*, edited by Gerald Markowitz and David Rosner. This is another collection of letters from government archives in which workers wrote to various government officials describing the conditions they faced in the work place. It is also an excellent collection.[12]

These studies are valuable and little of substance could be added to them. There is, however, an element of public opinion as expressed through letter-writing that none of them deal with very thoroughly. That is the almost obsessive desire of the people, both famous and obscure, to communicate with their president through verse. The amount of poetry, parody, and doggerel that Roosevelt received simply was overwhelming.

The use of poetry was not new in the Great Depression. Poetry, as a literary form, was read by most literate people in the early history of the nation. It had been used throughout history to express opinions to elected officials, especially presidents. Political songs, a form of poetry set to music, have long been a feature of our political system as well. Songs are more widely known since they often have been used in political campaigns. Lincoln, perhaps more than others, was written about in verse. Among the more famous tributes to Lincoln were the two poems by Walt Whitman, "O Captain! My Captain!" and "When Lilacs Last in the Courtyard Bloom'd." Poetry praising Lincoln came from the general public as well.[13]

Today's readers may be surprised that so many people resorted to verse to express their opinions. Today, poetry is not a popular literary form, certainly not like it was in the nineteenth century. Even before World War II poetry was still a viable and somewhat popular form of literature among the general public. Only after World War II did poetry lose its general audience and become largely an academic enterprise. Lucas Carpenter has written an excellent brief article on the current state of poetry and briefly summarized what happened to poetry as peoples' literature.

Carpenter explains that before the war a sizable number of outlets that the general public read still existed. According to Carpenter, poets could still "scratch out a living writing poetry. . . . An extensive magazine market served a wide, dependable audience for mostly popular poetry."[14] Thus, the average person in the 1930s read more poetry than people do today. Poetry was not considered an intellectual or academic subject. Though it may have been sentimental and simple in structure, poetry appealed to people who found reading to be a pleasurable activity. Poetry was common enough in a person's life that it was not uncommon for people to try writing verses themselves. Thus, people in the pre-World War II era would not have felt self-conscious or embarrassed to write poetry to express their political views. To send such poetry to a public official was not unusual.

Writing poetry to public officials probably still exists to some extent, but it is almost extinct. As a part of this study, all other presidential libraries were contacted to determine if they had collections of poetry from average citizens similar to those held by the Hoover and Roosevelt libraries. All presidential libraries responded to say that they had no comparable collections and that poetry was not a major subject heading of correspondence received from citizens throughout the country. If poetry exists in these libraries, it is scattered in the many files of those repositories and is not easily found.

The thing that makes the use of poetry and songs so unusual in the 1930s was the extent to which they were used. The Roosevelt Library in Hyde Park has at least forty manuscript boxes filled with poetry received by Roosevelt after he became president. Another forty boxes or so contain music, both published and unpublished, written about Roosevelt or one or more of his New Deal programs. In addition to these specialized collections one finds poetry scattered throughout almost all of the papers in the Roosevelt Library. One of the most useful, yet difficult to use, is the collection of papers from the Democratic National Committee for the four years before Roosevelt became president, 1928-1933. The study of poetry in this collection is difficult because the correspondence is organized chronologically by states, and the entire collection runs to more than 800 manuscript boxes.

A person who studies poetry of the depression must also take into account the correspondence received by President Herbert Hoover. The Hoover Library does not have any collections comparable to the poetry and music collections or anything similar to the Democratic National Committee files for the Republican Party. Nonetheless, Hoover received many poems, and the library is organized in such a way that a very thorough sampling of this type of public opinion can be made.

The poetry and songs received by Hoover and Roosevelt are of various quality. A small part was written by professionals and can thus be considered of reasonably good literary quality. Most of the material, however, was written by average people who were more concerned about expressing an opinion or offering praise than they were about the literary quality of their work. Some of the poetry was published in newspapers or magazines and some was printed as broadsides, leaflets, or postcards at the authors' expense. Most of it was written by hand or typed, sometimes rather poorly. Whatever its form, the poetry expressed the feelings of a large segment of the American public.

The poetry falls into several distinct categories. Much of it was merely praise for Hoover or Roosevelt. These poets mostly were interested in expressing their gratitude to their leaders for things they had done. Admittedly, Roosevelt received much more of the laudatory poetry than did Hoover, partly because he was in office longer and partly because his programs were more innovative and far-reaching. Many of the pro-Roosevelt poems were also anti-Hoover in tone. Beyond the poems of personal praise, many of the verses commented on various aspects of each president's program; again this was more true of Roosevelt's New Deal. Many of the poems and songs were designed to advise the president to whom they were addressed. Others were meant as encouragement, and some were extremely critical.

The goal of this study is to demonstrate and analyze public sentiment about the depression and the programs of Presidents Hoover and Roosevelt as expressed by the people through poetry. This study will show that the poets (both professional and amateur) of America reacted in pretty much the same fashion and in the same proportion as the general public to the economic and social crisis of the depression and the various actions taken to cope with it. The poets should be considered as a representative sampling of the American people; they are one segment of the public who expressed their views in a somewhat unique way. The opinions expressed in verse follow closely the views expressed by letter writers as shown in the other studies mentioned above.

This study is not literary criticism and is not designed to judge the literary quality of the poetry written during the depression. The major objective here is to analyze the opinion expressed through this medium about the social and political issues of the day. The poets believed that their views would be more easily heard and more quickly read if they were written in an unusual fashion. Little did they realize that so many people were doing the same thing that it no longer was unusual or unique.

The amateur poets of the depression era were not self-conscious about the form in which they wrote their opinions. In fact, many of the poets mentioned that they had previously had poetry published in local newspapers and other outlets. Sometimes they sent clippings from publications of the work they had done. Clearly, some of the correspondents were recognized in their communities as poets who were read regularly.

# 8 Poetry of the People

The people who wrote poetry during the depression cannot be categorized as a single type; persons of all ages, backgrounds, and levels of education wrote. Some of the poets told the president something about themselves while others were silent. Sometimes poems were sent by friends of the poets who may themselves have been too shy to promote themselves. Quite a number of the poets were elderly people and many of them made certain that the president knew their ages. Yet, many of the poets were school children, some as young as seven or eight years old. Some of the poets clearly were well-educated persons who had studied poetry and wrote well-crafted verses. Others were poorly educated and some were barely literate. Most who wrote verse had a knack for rhyme, even if they sometimes strained for good rhyming words. On some occasions, the poets sent photographs of themselves.

The people who wrote these poems are not always identified. Some poems were sent to Hoover or Roosevelt anonymously. A few poets used an older practice of writing under a pseudonym, often a Greek or Roman name. Even when the names are known, their place of residence is not always known. Few, if any, of the poets included in this work were known beyond their own families or communities. Names of the poets have not been included since they cannot all be identified, but they are identified by state or town and occupation when that is clear from the material. All poems are quoted exactly as written, including variations in spelling, capitalization, spacing, and punctuation.

Few of the poets would be still alive today, since these poems were written between fifty and sixty years ago. The letters and notes accompanying the poetry clearly indicates that the poets were adults—even elderly persons—who would not be alive today. Some of the poems were written by children and young adults who might still be alive. It would be interesting to contact them and know their reactions today to the poetry they wrote so long ago, but locating survivors is an impossible task.

Some of the poets wanted recognition for their work. Quite a number asked the presidents—usually Roosevelt—to use their influence to get their poems published or to get the poems set to music and used as campaign songs. They believed that their messages would be beneficial if only they could get their words before the public. Sometimes poets offered to share the royalties they would receive with the president's help, usually a favorite charity of the president. Many of the poets wanted the recognition that would come if their poetry could be set to music and played on the radio. Many of them mentioned that they could not afford to have musical scores written, but they were sure the president's influence could get it done.

The poetry that exists in both presidential libraries is truly peoples' poetry. It often is unsophisticated and the authors many times are clearly uneducated people. One might compare the poetry with amateur art. It might be considered "primitive" or "naive" art in verse form. One cannot read the poetry, especially in the original, without feeling some of the pain or suffering or happiness of the poet. The reader can see the care that went into the printing of the verses with pencil or pen and the difficulty some poets had in typing the poems. The paper on which the poetry and songs were written was of various types. Some were on lined tablets while others were on personalized, engraved stationary. Quite a number were written on the stationary provided by hotels. Some were written on scraps of paper while others were professionally printed and even included art work. A few were even printed in booklet or pamphlet form.

This study is designed for the general reading public as well as professional historians. The peoples' poetry from the Great Depression has been unknown far too long and this work is designed to make it known to the general reading public. To set the poetry in the context of the time in which it was written, it was necessary to explain some of the historical events that are generally well known. People who are not specialists in the 1930s might not understand the events or programs about which the poets were writing. Therefore, the professional will understand why the explanatory material is necessary.

Some consideration was given to publishing the poetry merely as an anthology. That approach was rejected, however, since this is not literary criticism. The goal of the study is to analyze the poetry for what it says about the events of the times. Therefore, a minimum amount of historical context was necessary for the poems to be understood as they would have been at the time had they been made available to the general public then.

The organization of the poetry was difficult. Many of the poems deal with many aspects of the depression. Some criticize Hoover and praise Roosevelt in the same poem. Others talk about several New Deal agencies in the same poem. Thus, the decision was made to organize this study topically. That may create some confusion as to chronology, but to have organized the material chronologically would have created even more confusion about the events of the time. The explanatory material attempts to set the topics in their proper chronological time frame.

A bit more information about organization may be helpful. The material was organized and chapters were selected based largely on the volume of poetry in the two collections on various topics.

Chapter 2 concentrates on Herbert Hoover and his administration. Hoover was elected in the midst of the great prosperity of the 1920s which was expected to continue. Poems of praise poured in on him during the election of 1928, extolling his past actions going back as far as World War I and continuing through his service as secretary of commerce in the 1920s. When the stock market crashed early in his administration in 1929, many of the poets wrote to tell him that he was not to blame and that the effects of the crash would be minimal. This was a period of attempted confidence building and denial that a depression actually existed. This followed the national trend.[15] Critics also began during this period.

Chapter 3 is concerned with the seriousness of the depression. Most of this poetry is concentrated in the early years of the depression, but some of it comes from poetry throughout the decade. Mostly, this chapter deals with the conditions people faced, as expressed by the poets.

The search for the cause of the depression is the subject of Chapter 4. In times of crisis, people always seek the cause—something on which to blame their misfortune. Many of the poets found the reason or reasons why they thought a depression existed.

Franklin Roosevelt was clearly the most important and controversial person of the 1930s. Chapter 5 focuses on the election of 1932 and the praise and support for Roosevelt. Since there were so many poems of praise for FDR, only a sampling is provided here. The poems of criticism are included in chapter 8.

Chapter 6 focuses on the various New Deal agencies that generated so much poetry. The poetry began immediately as the New Deal began and continued throughout the era. Most of the poetry regarding the agencies and programs were favorable, but there were some that were critical as well.

The depression era caused people to question the values on which America was based. Chapter 7 includes poems that deal with three major topics. One is the continuing issue of confidence which began in the aftermath of the stock market crash and continued through the depression decade. A second major issue poets discussed was the possibility of revolution during the depression. Included were the poets who praised and condemned socialism, fascism, and communism. The third matter of concern analyzed in this chapter was the pacifism and antiwar sentiment in America in the 1930s which lasted in many quarters until the outbreak of war in Europe in 1939 and American entry in 1941. All three of these topics are reviewed for the entire depression period.

Chapter 8 focuses upon the poets who were critical of Roosevelt and the New Deal. Many of the poets were very personal in their attacks on Roosevelt. Issues dealt with by the poets included such things as the brain trust, the president's family, including especially his wife Eleanor, various government programs, and Roosevelt personally. The poems come from all periods of the 1930s.

In summary, this study is a look at the poetry written by all types of citizens to their presidents during one of the most traumatic periods in American history. From this we may learn more about the American people and how they coped with such a crisis.

# 2

# The Good Old Days

Herbert Hoover came to the White House in 1929 with more promise than probably any president in American history. He was the prototype of the Horatio Alger story. Born of poor Quaker parents in the heartland of America, Iowa, he was orphaned at a tender age. Following his upbringing by various relatives he attended college at Stanford where he trained as an engineer.[1]

By the time he reached his forties he was a millionaire several times over. He had achieved the dream of so many Americans. He was rich enough that he never had to worry again about his future. At the same time, he was still young enough to devote his energies to making the world a better place in which to live.

What an enviable position! The parallel between his life and that of Andrew Carnegie is striking. However, where Carnegie did his good works through the donation of libraries and other philanthropic activities, Hoover turned his energies toward government service. Even though they took different paths toward service, they shared similar philosophical positions. Both were products of Social Darwinism—the philosophy that told them they succeeded because they were the fittest. In fact, if one follows the logic to its obvious conclusion, neither of them could have prevented himself from being successful. Thus, Hoover, like Carnegie, was a product of the school of rugged individualism that took a passive view of government that would allow each indvidual to achieve to the level of his own ability. Thus, Hoover was a follower of Jefferson's dictum that "the best government is that which governs least."

The end of the decade of the 1920s seemed a propitious time for a man of such views to assume the highest office in the land. The 1920s had been a decade of retreat from the activist policies of the New Freedom of Woodrow Wilson. Under Harding and Coolidge, the federal government and the presidency, as much as possible, had reverted to the philosophy that existed in the late nineteenth century. The reform movement was overshadowed by the new eminence of business—especially big business.

Herbert Hoover had been an integral part of this decade. True, he had started his public career as a part of the Wilson administration. His involvement with a Democrat as head of a federal agency that gave away food to war-torn Europe had caused him to be forever suspect by the most hardcore conservative Republicans. To most members of the party his eight years of service under Harding and Coolidge as Secretary of Commerce had pretty well erased that odious past. His service in the Commerce Department had been so successful that he was often labeled "the best Secretary of Commerce."

For Hoover to move into the presidency in 1929 seemed the most logical thing possible. For the country as a whole the future seemed very bright. The prosperity of the past decade would undoubtedly continue for at least eight more years under Hoover.

Hoover also may well be the most unfortunate president in our history. Coming into office in the wake of unprecedented prosperity and confidence, he found himself confronting the most profound economic depression in our history. Hoover's situation was even more sad because his entire personal background and philosophy made him totally unsuited to face this crisis. In truth, his presidency may be labeled an American tragedy.

The disappointment and discouragement—indeed, the tragedy—was to come after he had achieved the highest office in the land. Prior to that time he offered nothing but hope and confidence in the future.

As Hoover became a possible candidate for the Republican Party in 1928—especially after Calvin Coolidge made his famous statement that he did not choose to run—the poets of America began to remember Hoover's past service, especially in World War I, and to eulogize him for his contributions. His humble birth was extoled and various efforts were made to compare him to the first Republican president, Abraham Lincoln.

A humble beginning has never seemed to harm a presidential candidacy. As one poet said:

> It was in a log cabin Herbert Hoover was born,
> He plowed a straight furrow and hoed his own corn.
> He grew to be a man among men who feared God and Eschewed Evil
> For he had sand in his soul to acquit himself valiantly for his people.[2]

Especially important to the poets were his activities in Europe. Even after more than a year in the presidency, with all the problems that involved, a resident of New Jersey dug through his belongings and found a poem that somewhat symbolized American thinking at the time Hoover was in charge of Belgian relief.

> My Tuesdays are meatless, my Wednesday are wheatless,
>> I'm growing more eatless each day.
> My home, it is heatless, my bed it is sheetless,
>> They're all sent to Y. M. C. A.
> My club rooms are treatless, my coffee is sweetless,
>> Each day I grow simpler and wiser,
> My socks, they are feetless, my trousers are seatless,
>> My God! How I do hate the Kaiser![3]

The poet was not resentful of Hoover; he blamed the Kaiser for the sacrifices that Americans had to make to keep Europe alive. In fact, Hoover became a hero during that period and his name became symbolic with saving and scrimping. At the end of World War I, to "Hooverize" was a patriotic endeavor; in the 1930s "Hooverizing" became a term of scorn. "Hooverizing" was something he could be proud of.

> In the days of bloody war time,
> War which started o'er the water;
> In the days when Belgians suffered,
> Suffered from the pangs of hunger,
> Herbert Hoover was appointed
> With instructions to relieve them,
> To relieve them by some method,
> Any method of his choosing.
> How he did it, all remember;
> All remember of the coining
> Of the word called "Hooverizing."
> All the people of our nation
> Fell in line and gave assistance,
> Eating war bread, growing gardens,
> Giving up their meat and sugar,
> Shipping it across the water,
> Skimping that the mighty Hoover
> Could accomplish thus his purpose.
> This was done without complaining;
> Glad we were that we could do it.
> So he fed the starving Belgians,
> Fed them with the aid of millions;

By that aid became a hero
And the high and mighty None Such.[4]

A person who could organize relief the way Hoover could, and a
person so concerned with human suffering, was obviously the man to be
president. As a resident of Salt Lake City put it:

Hoover was the laddie, who sailed across the seas!
Underneath the Stars and Stripes floating on the breeze!
To feed the hungry millions and see they didn't freeze!
He's the man we got to have for President![5]

Hoover's reputation as the savior of Europe came back to haunt him
when he steadfastly refused to provide direct relief to the starving of
America. But before those events occurred the image of a humanitarian
was played to its limit. In fact, Hoover's extreme partisans probably did
him no good when they painted him as a virtual superman. That was
certainly the impression presented in the following five verses of a song
preserved today in the Hoover Library.

When the cannons were aroaring,
When the airplanes were asoaring,
When the skies were very dark
And of light there was no spark. . . .
　　Who made the horizon bright?
　　Who became its beacon light?--HOOVER!

When everyone was on the run,
When men's hearts turned to stone,
When to escape there was no place
And to appeal—no friendly face. . . .
　　Who day and night was busy?
　　Who made life more easy?--HOOVER!

When the people cried for bread,
When rebuffs they got instead,
When they suffered cold and hunger
And couldn't stand it any longer. . . .
　　Who got for the starving food?
　　Who found for the freezing wood?--HOOVER!

When friend and foe pained, ached,
When their bodies diseases, raked,
When no succor was in sight
And no relief for their plight. . . .
    Who got help for their need?
    Who cared naught for race or creed?--HOOVER!

When the East had no more food,
When their people were naked, nude,
When the world was weeping, crying
And mankind was starving, dying. . . .
    Who all of himself to others gave?
    Who saved millions from the grave?--HOOVER![6]

Sometimes the poets' logic or knowledge of history was slightly lacking, but that did not stifle their ardor as evidenced by the following lines:

We fed them our Armies,
We fed them our cash;
But Hoover's the man
That kept handing 'em hash,
And brought home the bacon
From Old Germany; (he is a 2 & 2 are 4 man)[7]

Others simply painted him as a great man as was the case in this campaign song of 1928.

Hoo! Hoo! Hoo! Hoorah for Hoover,
The man hoo sent our money over,
Hoo oversaw the buying
Of food to save the dying
In Europe's needy, starving multitoode,
In Europe's needy, starving multitoode.

Hoo! Hoo! Hoo! Hoorah for Hoover,
Hoo of great forces is the mover,
Hoo wooed and won our giving
Too help the world keep living--
He's worthy of our hearty gratitoode,
He's worthy of our hearty gratitoode.[8]

Other than the hero worship that was evident here, America's bards also saw his service as an example of the executive leadership that America needed above all else to see her through the next eight years. In a poem advocating Hoover's election the poet castigated the Democrats and then had this to say:

> They don't want to hear anybody tell
>     Of the many big jobs he's done mighty well:
> As an Executive, no man is your peer--
>     Your Ability, Sir, is the thing they fear.[9]

Not only was Hoover's executive and administrative ability evident in his wartime service; as Secretary of Commerce he proved to be the man of the hour. In concert with Secretary of the Treasury Andrew Mellon, he did everything he could to make American business successful and prosperous. The Commerce Department was used in a very aggressive way to prove Coolidge's statement, "The business of America is business."

In addition, as Secretary of Commerce, Hoover's humanitarian reputation was further enhanced. When a disastrous flood occurred on the Mississippi River Hoover moved quickly into action to bring the resources of the government to the aid of the destitute. Later when the depression harmed far more bodies and souls he would again be accused of being inconsistent in philosophy. For him, however, there was no inconsistency. The flood was an act of God that its victims could not prevent; government assistance to them was, therefore, logical and necessary. However, the victims of the depression—far more in number —were somehow responsible for their own fate and should not be helped directly by the federal government.

In the years before he became president, he was, nonetheless, regarded as the ultimate humanitarian. Thus, the poets and songwriters extolled his virtues to the limit. One poet put it this way:

> He was recognized as a saver at home and abroad,
> When millions were threatened by famine or flood,
> By his Master Mind impending dangers were controlled,
> And stormy billows ceased to roll o'er a nation's peaceful soul.[10]

Or as another one said:

> In the flood and in the war when our country's needs were sore,
> There this master mind and leader took a hand.

> And the People now proclaim from North to South from West to
> Maine.
> Herbert Hoover--Herbert Hoover is the man.[11]

One of the 1928 songwriters made him appear to be a superman—an image that no doubt would have embarrassed the modest Hoover if he knew of the song.

> He's a master of emergencies well known thru-out the land,
> When ever trouble has appeared he's there with helping hand,
> Thru famine and thru fire and flood at home or 'cross the sea,
> He's ever ready on the job to help humanity.[12]

Emphasizing Hoover's humanitarian and superhuman efforts in the flood the songwriter put it this way:

> When Mississippi River--chose to overflow, and take--
> A toll of human lives--leaving sadness in it's wake--
> Herbert Hoover was the man elected for the case--
> He fed the poor--relieved the pain--put that river back in
> place.[13]

As Hoover went into the campaign of 1928 things could not have looked better. In addition to being something of a minor national hero, he was also facing a Democratic Party going through its periodic infighting. Alfred Smith, the governor of New York, was so distasteful a candidate to some that portions of the "Solid South" voted Republican for the first time since Reconstruction. The issues of Smith's Catholicism, his stand as a "wet" during a time of national prohibition, and the problem of his city ways in attracting rural voters have been thoroughly analyzed by others and need not be repeated here.

These campaign issues did not attract the poets very much. Since there are no collections for the Democrats in this year, one might assume that poetry was written dealing with these topics. If one is to judge from the poems available in the Hoover Library, however, other things aroused the minds of the poets.

For example, they continued to emphasize Hoover's record.

> Hoover's There--Always There--
> When he's needed he always is there;
> If it's foods or famine, or rivers dammin'
> Then Hoover's needed everywhere.

> Over Here--Over There;
> All the world is for Herb 'cause he's fair.
> Put him over--We'll be in clover
> When our country's calling Hoover
> HOOVER'S There.[14]

Most of the poetry was laudatory in nature and did not deal with specific issues. It seemed enough to them to show Hoover's record and to expect the public to respond accordingly.

> It was logic and truth and a rare foresight
> That pleaded his cause and gained him the right
> To feed the starving and save the might
>     Of a perishing race.
>
> 'Twas the hardest task a man can know;
> But he gained men's trust, and even the foe
> Let him freely come and go,
>     As no one else.
>
> He did it all with no reward,
> Except a world's undying laud.
> He is our own. With one accord
>     We hail him chief.[15]

One amateur poet from Iowa did try to dissect the Democrats on the issues. He systematically attacked the Democrats in verse for their stand on prohibition, the farm issue, the tariff, and labor policy. He concluded:

> Their platform is a hodge-podge,
>     And a conglomeration,
> But its' plainly apparent
>     'Twill not fool the nation.
>
> It's supremely absurd,
>     And causes a laugh;
> Think you they'll win votes
>     With nothing but chaff?[16]

Then in a reference to the influence of the Tammany Hall "tiger" on Smith he made a further statement that to him seemed utterly unnecessary.

Let the big tiger roar,
    And the mad donkey bray,
Hoover and Curtis will win,
    Sure as night follows day.[17]

Much of the poetry and most of the songs were the usual campaign type material that said very little and were aimed at arousing the emotions of the voters rather than dealing with the issues. An example was the campaign song entitled "Hoover! We Want Hoover!" which said, in part:

He's the right man to succeed our president Cal Coolidge,
Hoover's an executive and has tremendous knowledge;
Presidents Republican, have brought progress to our land,
If good times you wish to see, Line up with the G.O.P.[18]

There were also those who wished to join in the crusade but really did not know how. An example of this type of poetry or doggerel or whatever it might be called is the following:

ROCK OF AGES: CLIFT FOR ME:

LET ME HIDE IN HOOVER TREE

\*\*\*\*\*\*\*\*\*\*\*\*\*\*\*\*\*\*\*\*\*\*\*\*\*\*\*\*\*\*\*

ROCK OF AGES CLIFT FOR RAN

LET ME EAT AT HOOVER STAND

\*\*\*\*\*\*\*\*\*\*\*\*\*\*\*\*\*\*\*\*\*\*\*\*\*\*\*\*\*\*\*

ROCK OF AGES CLIFT FOR ME

LET HOOVER BEND HIS BEND NEE

\*\*\*\*\*\*\*\*\*\*\*\*\*\*\*\*\*\*\*\*\*\*\*\*\*\*\*\*\*\*\*

ROCK OF AGES: CLIFT FOR NELL

LET ME LODGE AT HOOVER HOTEL

\*\*\*\*\*\*\*\*\*\*\*\*\*\*\*\*\*\*\*\*\*\*\*\*\*\*\*\*\*\*\*

ROCK OF AGES CLIFT FOR LIFE:

HOPE TO MEAT HOOVER AND WIFE

\*\*\*\*\*\*\*\*\*\*\*\*\*\*\*\*\*\*\*\*\*\*\*\*\*\*\*\*\*\*\*

ROCK OF AGES CLIFT FOR LAR:

LET ME RIDE IN HOOVER CARR

\*\*\*\*\*\*\*\*\*\*\*\*\*\*\*\*\*\*\*\*\*\*\*\*\*\*\*\*\*\*\*

ROCK OF AGES CLIFT FOR RAY

WE BEE THAIR ON LECTION DAY

\*\*\*\*\*\*\*\*\*\*\*\*\*\*\*\*\*\*\*\*\*\*\*\*\*\*\*\*\*\*\*

ROCK OF AGES CLIFT FOR RAN
HOPE TO BEE AT HOOVER HAND
\*\*\*\*\*\*\*\*\*\*\*\*\*\*\*\*\*\*\*\*\*\*\*\*\*\*\*\*\*\*\*\*\*\*[19]

Although this piece is not very good, it was a hint of what was to come as the years passed. This person obviously had a feeling for Hoover that he tried to express. It may well have also been an attempt to be a part of something.

On another note an amateur poet dealt with what to him was a major campaign issue in "The Hog Question." He said that the election of Smith would spell doom to the hog business for it "will die like a rotten tree."[20] Hoover, he believed, was a strong man who would be able to keep the hog raiser in business. He also believed that various hog diseases were destroying the business, but this could be corrected by the use of medicine produced by himself. His logic is somewhat twisted but he was able to tie Hoover's election to the use of his hog remedy.

Cast your vote for Hoover and be a man
For greater prosperity all over the land
Fine fat hogs on every farm you will see
That has been treated with Smokey's never failing remedy[21]

Even though Hoover came to the presidency in the midst of great prosperity, in less than eight months he was faced with the stock market crash of October 1929 and the resulting loss of confidence. An administration that had promised to be a continuation of the status quo now became one besieged by a crisis greater than any domestic period in our past. Hoover, the so-called "Great Engineer," now had to deal with the human tragedy, a problem for which his past had not prepared him.

During this period of unhappiness for Hoover, numerous people around the country stayed with him and occasionally tried to cheer him up. The efforts of the poets took several directions.

For example, there were those who tried to exude the confidence that Hoover urged everyone to have. From the beginning Hoover had repeated that the economy of the nation was sound; the problem was that people might lose confidence and the country would suffer.

As early as 1930 Hoover was told that the depression was just about over and that good times were coming again.

We showed the world
That we could fight

Even without gain

So come on--let's go
Tell everyone you know
GOOD TIMES ARE COMING AGAIN.

Let's all get together
And see what we can do
GOOD TIMES ARE COMING AGAIN.[22]

This poet did not offer any suggestions or reasons why times were changing; she simply had faith. Another one said that all the people had to do was try.

We can whip this old depression
    All we have to do is try
So start smileing, quit all blameing
    See how jolly you can be
And before you even know it
    We will have prosperity--[23]

Perhaps, as some said, confidence was all that was needed. Prosperity was the natural condition of America, and Hoover's leadership was the answer.

Yes, Hoover's at the Helm
    Of our good old Ship of State,
And will land her in the Harbor,
    With all her precious freight,

With her store of golden grain
    And her products of the loom,
As the Nation's blood is tingling
    With Prosperity's rich boom.[24]

Another one said on the eve of the 1932 election that Hoover had ended the depression.

Hurrah, the depression is over
Tis the dawn of a glorious day
Shout loud your praise for our leader
Hoover has shown us the way[25]

A cynic might conclude that most of these people were whistling in the dark to keep themselves from being afraid of the unknown and forces they could not control. One poet, however, believed that there was really no depression.

> The government's got to do something
> Or we'll fall in our tracks and there lay
> Yet the woman, who does up our wash
> Brings it back in a yellow coupe.[26]

In fact, he believed that people were deliberately scared by the Democrats to discredit Hoover. Several verses in his poem imply that money is available and that people will spend it for entertainment such as movies, ball games, or prize fights, and still complain about hard times. How widely his conclusion was held by the public is difficult to determine.

> So all of this talk of a panic
> Of the country about to go "flunk"
> Between you and me and the toastmaster
> Is a lot of damn Democrat "bunk".[27]

As conditions worsened and suffering became more severe, the criticism of Hoover mounted. The defenders of Hoover became so upset by what they considered to be unwarranted attacks that they rushed to his defense in rhyme. A series of poems, some quite humorous in nature, were written to try to show that the attacks were unjust. Space will allow only a sampling of these poems here. One such poem was sent to a Vermont newspaper, but the editor considered it "a little too tart for a family publication."[28] Instead he sent it on to the White House hoping that the president might get a chance to see it.

> I have some corns upon my feet,--
>     Herb Hoover is to blame.
> A recent cyclone wrecked our street,--
>     Herb Hoover is to blame.
> My crop of beans is very small,
> My onions didn't grow at all,
> The rats are in my cellar wall,
>     Herb Hoover is to blame!

I find my eyes are growing dim,--
    Herb Hoover is to blame,
My cross-eyed girl is weak and slim,--
    Herb Hoover is to blame.
My oldest boy is running booze,
And little Jimmy smokes and chews,
I'm nearly dying of the blues,
    Herb Hoover is to blame![29]

Another example came from Wisconsin.

He is the source of all our grief,
The fount of all our woe;
We've come at last to that belief
We know that it is so;
The darksome days that now are here,
Are all Herb Hoover's fault
He brought the whole dern thing about,
He isn't worth his salt.[30]

An Iowan also came to Hoover's defense.

Does the wolf howl at your door?
              Jump on Hoover!
Are your prospects rather poor?
              Land on Hoover!
Does your husband sometimes snore?
Is your wife a tiresome bore?
Are your bunions awf'ly sore?
              Kick at Hoover![31]

Occasionally, a poet had to stretch hard to find words that rhymed. Even though the word "pelf" is legitimate, it is not often used and seemed contrived.

If you have no God but the god of pelf
And are not ashamed of your ornery self,
    Lay it on to Hoover.
Hunt up all the silly things men plan or manuever
From Halifax to Tia Juana, from Havana to Vancouver,
    And lay them all on to Hoover.[32]

There were some poets who were quite knowledgeable about technical matters. In the following selection potential readers probably would not have known that pip is a poultry disease and a bot is an insect that infects cattle. Most would probably have concluded that the poet was coining words for his own convenience.

> If the chicks in the hen house all died of the pip,
> If your best girl went high-hat and gave you the slip,
> If you fell down the stairs - dislocated your hip -
> > Blame Hoover.
> Did the cows get the bots? Did the dog get the mange?
> Did the coy-o-tes kill all the sheep on the range?
> That is proof that what's needed right now is a change -
> > Defeat Hoover[33]

This poem was from a disabled veteran from Tacoma, Washington. He told the president that he was right not to give in to the veterans' demand for their bonus. He also said that he wrote his poem because, "It sometimes happens that a thing of this sort will have more influence, in some places, than the most logical and straight forward exposition of facts."[34] He also explained to Hoover that he was trying to get the poem published in a newspaper. Whether he did is not known.

These people who were attempting a bit of poetic satire did not limit themselves to "blaming" Hoover for all domestic troubles. He was also "to blame" for world events. According to the author of this poem, the poem from which the following is only a selection actually changed chronic critics into Hoover boosters in several instances when they read it in a local newspaper in Wisconsin.

> He is to blame for Japanese
> Invading lands they do not own;
> For starving millions overseas,
> He is to blame, it can be shown.[35]

Another poet said it this way:

> When there's turmoil in China, revolt in Brazil,
> And the troubles of Russia, the newspapers fill,
> When England cant find any gold in her till -
> > Jump on Hoover.
> When Germany riots, and Italy stews,

And the Czhechs and Slovaks cannot buy any shoes,
When the Japs all go nuts, as though full of bum booze -
             Pick on Hoover.[36]

As the criticism of Hoover intensified there were those among his supporters who feared that he might become discouraged and lose hope. For them, this would have been to admit defeat. One of his supporters felt that the president needed a bit of bolstering up.

What's a bump or two? Just laugh!
Pull a grin and stand tha gaff!
Prove that you're too good a man
To be just an 'also ran';
Tie to this when times are tough---
DO YOUR STUFF, KID; DO YOUR STUFF![37]

Many people felt that Hoover should be pictured as a brave man who guided the nation through a turbulent course even while he was taking the slings and arrows of the Democrats and other opponents. The analogy of Hoover as the captain of a ship was common.

Now the seas once more are stormy and the angry waters rage,
    While the Ship of State is tossing where depression battles
      wage;
Captain Hoover, brave and fearless, stands undaunted at the
    wheel,
    With clear and steadfast purpose, trying to keep an even keel.

Never wavering, nor relaxing, for no rest he can afford;
    All around the battle rages and there's mutiny on board.
These are all uncharted waters, where no craft has sailed before;
    The whole world is in a turmoil and the storm strikes every
      shore.[38]

Others tried to show that he was the tower of strength that the nation needed.

Hoover our guide through this darkness
Endowed by the spirit above
Stands at the helm of the nation
A tower of strength much beloved

> Trust him I beg all our people
> He has Fathered numerous bills
> That will prove beyond all suspicion
> He has cures for all of our ills[39]

A woman from Michigan approached Hoover in the same manner.

> High above the quibbling, scurrying mob
> A heroic figure stands in thoughtful calm;
> Untouched by greed or petty vanities of life;
> A man whom history will not dare deny![40]

Some of Hoover's defenders tried to picture him as not caring about what the people said about him; instead he was only interested in doing what was right and in bringing the country through the depression.

> For he has sought the world to save,
> From desolation deep and grave.
> Unmindful of the sneers and taunts,
> Sent forth from arrows poisoned darts:
> Unmindful of the coarse crowd's jeers,
> Unflinching through that crowd he steers
> Serene, he answers a duty's call,
> To keep erect that none may fall[41]

Therefore, he is still the same hardworking man that he always was, unchanged by the burdens he has to bear.

> When things look bare, he's always there
>     Working hard at the game,
> And so today, when clouds are gray,
>     We find him just the same.[42]

Hoover was sure that history would vindicate him.

> He eats and sleeps the same as us,
>     Gets hungry and gets tired,
> And gets the same old blame as us
>     (And usu'ly it's wired),
> But folks are slow at praising him,
>     The same as you and me—

Yet neither one is fazing him,
     As far as I could see.

He's just a plain American,
     As plain as all the rest,
And taking all the care he can
     To do his level best--
Views enemies with charity,
     And friendship with delight,
Because he knows posterity
     Will say that he was right.[43]

To blame Hoover was absurd his supporters believed. He was no more responsible for the depression than anyone else. He was, they believed, doing more than anyone to end it. Certainly, the Democrats were simply taking advantage of the situation to embarrass him. This view was expressed crudely by one man from St. Louis:

We have Blamed Our President
As the cause of all our Luck
     That is Childish Foolisheness
Its just, "Passing the Buck

. . . . . . . . . . . . . . .
     It is'nt Mr. Hoover's Fault
That times are like they are
     Its the Same all over
In lands near and Far.[44]

A resident of Massachusetts explained it this way:

The times are under par today, we know the reason why,
And none can fix the blame on you no matter how they try;
We know you've done your level best to get us safely by
          So we will vote for you.          Chorus.

The times could not be better had your place been filled by "Cal",
Just think what might have happened if instead of you 't were
     "Al",
So we are duly grateful and we'll stand beside you, pal,
          On next election day.          Chorus.

> The democrats may blame you for the deeper tint of blue,
> The floods that ravished China and the drought that struck Peru,
> And other acts of Providence that none can lay to you,
>          But we can undertand.          Chorus.[45]

A Texan summed it up this way:

> Of all men most ignorant,
> When ignorance is supreme;
> The one that blames the President,
> His ignorance is the cream.[46]

Who or what was the cause of the depression? This question is serious enough and was the subject of so much poetry that it will have a whole chapter to itself. But if the cause was not Hoover, what then did his supporters believe to be the cause? One Kentuckian believed it was someone else:

> It Is'nt Mr. Hoover's Fault
> Because You Can't Find Work,
> Tis The Men Who Invent The Machinery,
> Who Knock Thousands Out of Work.[47]

A woman from California was convinced that it was not Hoover. However, in discussing the Democrats ("Bourbons" she called them) one wonders how early the beginnings were since Republicans had controlled the White House for more than ten years.

> "Dire calamity" the Bourbons always shout,
> "Turn us in and we will turn the rascals out;"
> But 'twas when they had their innings
> That depression had its beginnings,
> We propose now to keep those rascals out.[48]

This woman was very generous to the president. She said she was still unemployed but she did not blame that on Hoover. Really, all she could see as the cause were the Democrats.

As poets tried to mollify the impact of the depression there were those who went further. They were such strong supporters of Hoover that they believed his reputation would compare with giants from the past.

For example, one New Yorker, in a poem entitled "The Three Engineers," compared Hoover with Napoleon (the Corsican) and George Washington.

> Our age in nineteen thirty restless seethes,
> Aftermath of great war oer old world plain;
> Once more sage engineer doth rule, but grieves
> Oer woes which our fair lands and others stain.
> Like Washington, serves meek our land and world
> Both day and night, which all are peoples own;
> Unlike great Corsican who war bolts hurl'd,
> He works and acts ere glory's fame is known.[49]

Another compared him to Moses and to George Washington. Both Moses and Washington, he said, were leaders of people who mocked them and did not appreciate them at the time. But both men led their people through the dark days to victory and were proclaimed as heroes. Undoubtedly, he believed, Hoover would be the same.

> Herbert Hoover saw the turmoil
> That would smite the land with woe,
> As did everyone with foresight,
> But he did not fear the blow,
>
> And he chose to lead his people.....
> And withstood their mocks and jeers.
> He will rank with George and Moses,
> Victorious, in the coming years.[50]

Other compared him with Abraham Lincoln. Both Hoover and Lincoln were faced with domestic crises of serious proportions. Both had to make decisions that would affect the country for years to come.

> We have another Lincoln down in Washington
> His name is Herbert Hoover he's loved by everyone
> We'll keep him in the white House for the good work he has done
> We have another Lincoln down in Washington[51]

A woman from Utah compared them favorably.

> He stands
> As Abraham Lincoln stood long years ago,
> His country with war's open wound to heal,

Surrounded by ambitious countrymen,
Yet giving even life for an ideal.
When mists have rolled away and veils are rent,
When eyes bedimmed shall have a vision new,
With heads erect, hand clasped in hand
But silhouetted against heavenly blue
These two shall stand.[52]

Another woman compared Hoover to a gardener.

The gardner is equal to his many tasks;
But he needs time and faith - that's all he asks.
He knows that he has accomplished more
Than many folks give him credit for.
The weeds were growing when he started to work;
And the cutworms and earwigs were there in the dirt.
He is ridding the garden of enemies of life,
And asks for the chance to settle more strife.
When the flowers droop, his big heart aches;
And he'd gladly give all - though his life it takes -
To restore this garden and it's beauty once more,
So the whole world will admire - as never before.[53]

Hoover received other types of praise during his term that cannot be classified as poetry. It was common for a person to use various words, especially the president's name, to praise him. One example is the following:

**H** ail to the Chief of the Nation,
**E** mblem of power, of right;
**R** ender him highest oblation,
**B** eacon of undieing light.
**E** nter his name on that portal
**R** eared by the wisdom of men
**T** here to be numbered Immortal

**H** onor the Chief of the Nation
**O** nly as leader and friend
**O** , may his administration
**V** indicate love that will blend!
**E** ver the voice that he raises
**R** adiates plaudits and praises.[54]

Here is another one of this type.

HERBERTC.HOOVER-*-*-*-*-*-*-*-*-*-*-

| | | |
|---|---|---|
| H | Heroic in his effort | H |

-----------------------------

| | | |
|---|---|---|
| E | Earnest in all he dares, attempts | E |

******************

| | | |
|---|---|---|
| R | Robust and radiant his smile | R |

-----------------------------

| | | |
|---|---|---|
| B | Benificence his makeup claims | B |

*******************

| | | |
|---|---|---|
| E | Efficiency his watchword is | E |

-----------------------------

| | | |
|---|---|---|
| R | Religious he that modest type | R |

*******************

| | | |
|---|---|---|
| T | Trustful, hopeful with patience, reserve | T |

-----------------------------

| | | |
|---|---|---|
| C. | Character, marked and capable | C |

******************

| | | |
|---|---|---|
| H | Heroic again, I pronounce him | H |

-----------------------------

| | | |
|---|---|---|
| O | Oratory in him as posessed | O |

*******************     *

*******************     *

| | | |
|---|---|---|
| O | Old fashioned traits in him admired | O |

-----------------------------

| | | |
|---|---|---|
| V | Venerably, valiantly he stands | V |

******************

| | | |
|---|---|---|
| E | Emenent he as an engineer | E |

-----------------------------

| | | |
|---|---|---|
| R | Realist, ready to reverently Serve | R |

******************

\*     (-First line stanza verses-)        \*
HERBERTC.HOOVER-*-*-*-*-*-*-*-*-[55]

The following one is interesting because of the reaction it created.

O ne who strives to do the best he can
U ndaunted by the woes and cares of man
R ugged as the rocks long-lashed by the sea

P repared to guide the Land, what e're may be
R eligious, for he knows he cannot lead alone
E steemed by all, he is our stepping stone
S incere as the old saying "True Blue"
I nstructing us in all that we attempt to do
D evoted to the Land he loves so true
E ndeavoring to make it a happy place for you
N oiselessly he goes about the tasks to be won
T iring not 'till every one assigned is done

H umbly he waits to answer your cry
O ne who has been taught "Never Say Die"
O wing the World nothing, he shows it the way
V anity is not in this great man of today
E nriching us with the confidence of a winner, not loser
R embering he is our leader, PRESIDENT HOOVER.[56]

When this was received in the White House the secretary to the president sent it to the Republican National Committee for possible use in publicity material. The response from the committee was an amusing tongue-in-cheek letter that undoubtedly reflected the opinion of many who handled the mail on a regular basis. The letter bears extensive quotation.

It is TERRIBLE!

Indeed that word doesn't begin to tell how bad it is. Read it over again. Read it out loud. Read it in cold blood. And then say whether you could print it yourself, if you were editing this high tone and dignified Weekly Letter. Seriously, what I fear is that two things would happen if I let it appear. One is that I should lose my reputation, and the other is that I should be flooded with similar outbreaks from all over the country. Long experience has taught me that nothing is so contagious as bad poetry. Seeing it thousands of people, mostly young girls, would say, "Why I can write as good a piece as that," and proceed forthwith to do it.[57]

Letters to Hoover containing poetry of one sort or another continued throughout his presidential term. The volume of all mail increased as the 1932 election neared. Much of the general correspondence, as well as the poetry already discussed, was concerned with strategy for the coming election. Virtually all of the poetry Hoover received was favorable to him. The critical and unflattering material went to Franklin D. Roosevelt and other Democrats. Since the election was such a crucial matter a major portion of this study will be devoted to it later.

Hoover, of course, faced odds in 1932 that would have been serious for any incumbent. For Hoover, the cold and aloof individual that he was, they were disastrous.

In the aftermath of the election some Americans remained loyal enough to Hoover to try to console him in his defeat.

> Not ours the victor's name to sing,
>> By million voices greeted;
> Today a rarer toast we bring,
>> A toast to one defeated.[58]

The number of people supporting Hoover in 1932 had dwindled to only a fraction of his great acclaim in 1928. Some were bitter about the defeat while others took a more philosophical attitude. The correspondence received by Hoover was primarily from hard-core supporters who refused to desert him or the banners of the Republican Party. By far, most of those who supported his opponent wrote their congratulations to Roosevelt. Often they included blistering attacks on Hoover for his action or inaction.

One woman from Montana who was also a leader in the prohibition movement told Hoover what kind of people Americans were.

> Oh, President Hoover, I grieve that it's true
> But this nation has proved
>> Most ungrateful to you;
> You have spent all your planning,
> Your prayers, and your time,
> Upon people whose ignorance
>> Seems almost sublime.[59]

Then she ended her poetic tribute by telling Hoover that he would be vindicated someday.

> Oh Captain! Herb Hoover!
> We'll all rue the day
> When from our proud "White House,"
>> You travel away;
> We wish you success
>> With the new job you choose,--

Your reward should be great
When God gives you your dues.[60]

Another woman told Hoover that although he had lost because of thoughtless voters, the lessons he taught had been learned by the thoughtful voters and would be continued.

So the horde of thoughtless voters,
Never counting up the Cost
Turned against our valiant Leader
And the cause of Right was lost.

Yet the thinking, helpful people
Will be staunch and kind and true,
And will carry on like Hoover
In whate'er there is to do.[61]

Some people did not dwell on the issues, but simply felt that Hoover should be honored for the service he had rendered even if a majority of Americans had rejected that leadership.

He toiled, he purposed, he attained.
    We dream of fields he planted,
We vision fairer prospects gained,
    Had time and patience granted.

The loss is ours - a lesser host,
    Disparaged and depleted,
We give again a ringing toast
    To one we love! Defeated.[62]

Another one said it this way:

But we, thy fellow citizens and friends,
Resolve that thou has nobly done thy best
And played a clear and honest role -
Preserved the nation in a world distressed
And earned the thanks of all thy countrymen.[63]

In the years after Hoover left the presidency, his reputation gradually recovered from the stigma of the depression until by the time of his death in the 1960s he had become something of a folk hero. In the immediate aftermath of his presidential service, however, Hoover remained a forgotten man to a major portion of the American electorate.

There was a loyal following even in these bleak years who believed that Hoover had been right all along and that history would vindicate him. Some maintained the forlorn hope that his political star might rise again in 1936 or 1940 and that he might have a chance to return to the White House. Such was not to be the case, however. The certainty of vindication was expressed by one woman this way:

> A man of vision, loving liberty.
>     A stateman worthy of the name.
> There is a quiet, secure nook
>     In human hearts and halls of fame
> For men like him—of his integrity.
>     And our historians will say
> He counseled wisely, in sincerity
>     To meet the crises of his day.[64]

The possibility of Hoover's reelection was expressed by one Kentuckian (apparently in 1935) this way:

> If anything is left next year
> Which I sometimes doubt and sometimes fear
> God grant Mr. Hoover may come back
> And Get us once more
> On the right track.[65]

Implicit in this selection is the suggestion that the programs of the Roosevelt New Deal had created more problems than they solved. If Herbert Hoover had remained in office the nation would not have faced these difficulties.

In the first stanza of the poem just quoted the gentleman from Kentucky expressed his feelings for both Hoover and Roosevelt:

> You had the country on the mend
> Had the depression near an end
> Had business on the upward trend
> By sane and normal methods when
> Franklin D. Roosevelt stepped in
> With His alphabetical brain trusters
> pledge breakers and promise busters[66]

An anonymous Florida woman expressed her dissatisfaction with Roosevelt's leadership and felt certain that the result would be a communist takeover. She was convinced that this would not have happened with Hoover. This poem is quoted in full.

> Who put the firecrackers under Spain,
> And started the strife on the Chink's terrain,
> And scattered the grasshoppers over the plain?
> Hoover?
>
> Who was it hoisted taxes high,
> To get the dough to hand to the guy
> Who wouldn't work to save an eye?
> Not Hoover!
>
> Who burned the wheat and killed the swine,
> And kicked the market in the spine,
> And yelled "Oh Boy, the world is mine"?
> Was it Hoover?
>
> Who was it taught that thrift is sin,
> And only bad men save their "tin",
> And when they squirm just looks, and grins,
> At Hoover?
>
> What with strikes and C. I. O.,
> And fireside chats by Radio;
> Ku Klux Judges and Heidy Ho,
> Lucky Hoover!
>
> But one day "when the well runs dry"
> And we nod to a Russian Lullaby,
> It'll be too late to rise and cry
> For a level headed
> Sort of Guy,
> Like Hoover.[67]

Another woman believed that Roosevelt's success and popularity were merely the result of Hoover's effort.

> You ask where we'd be in this dear U.S.A.
>     If Herbie were serving us yet?

We'd be sailing along on an unruffled sea
    On a boat not o'erladen with debt.
You say, "By their fruits ye shall know them." 'Tis so--
    Truer words never spoken by man,
For the flowers of prosperity F.R. now picks
    Are the buds which our Herbie began.[68]

Democrats continued to say during the 1930s that Hoover was finished politically. Some loyalists refused to give up, however. Such was the sentiment in the following poem about a conversation between "Kingfish" Huey Long and Hoover the Owl.

Said the Kingfish to the Owl,
Your're a downy old fowl,
But your day in the sun
Is done.
The times have changed,
And I have arranged
To show how the world should be run.
But the wise old bird
Said never a word,
As owls should always do.
Yet he winked his eye,
Which was meant to imply,
I'll be here when the Kingfish is through.[69]

As late as 1959 Hoover occasionally received tributes from people who admired him. The same general sentiments were expressed in the 1930s.

Beneath a mountain of abuse and lies,
    Which would demoralize even a saint,
HE would not yield or stoop to compromise
    His principles,--nor would his honor taint.
Though other leaders stole his wonder-plans,
    And set ward-heelers to malign his name,--
Though sabotaged by Envy and Mischance,
    HE would not cavil or return the blame.
like a blessing in a wicked world,
    He showered kindness and benevolence;
'Gainst Terror's path his strength and wealth he hurled,
    And strove to stem the Flood of Violence.

Here is a MAN for all to emulate,
A Beacon for the humble AND the great.[70]

Herbert Hoover, without question, was one of the major tragedies of the depression. Probably no other president was more scorned and villified during his lifetime. Even in death there are many people who still hold him personally responsible for the depression. The opinions of professional historians vary. Probably, it will still be some time before the final judgment of history is in.

Even so, Hoover had his defenders as well as detractors. Many tried to tell him of their feelings in verse even though much of it was really bad poetry. The quality was not important; people of all types told a beleagered man that they loved and trusted him, even if they were in a minority. The attacks will be discussed more fully in chapter 4.

# 3

## The Bleakness of Depression

Even though Herbert Hoover assumed the presidency on one of the greatest waves of hope and confidence in our history, his plans were wrecked in less than a year by the greatest economic depression this country had ever known. Hoover's reputation was destroyed, but the American people suffered even more.

Many of the unemployed, with little else to do, turned more and more to expressing their views in poetic form. They revealed the depth of depression. Most of the poets either blamed Hoover personally or praised Roosevelt for the efforts he made to ease the burdens of the common people. Interestingly, very few of the poets wrote specifically of how bad things were. Conditions of life were often merely assumed or alluded to in their efforts to place the blame for the debacle or in their confident statements about how things were improving under Roosevelt and his programs. Therefore, the student of the period has to look carefully at the poetry written with another purpose: to find descriptions of conditions American faced.

One woman from Spokane, Washington, did discuss how bad things were at the end of President Hoover's term. The relief she describes must have come from private charitable sources since Hoover did not approve of direct federal relief.

> When President Roosevelt came into the Chair
>     The country had gone to the dogs,
> The men out of work were losing their homes
>     And for meat, some were eating "green frogs."
> They had placed life's savings in banks that closed down,
>     And were walking the streets in despair,
> They were put on relief, given food, given clothes,
>     They were getting so they didn't care.[1]

An eleven-year-old girl from Philadelphia told President Roosevelt what a good job he had done in early 1936 as he entered a presidential year. Obviously, the child was more interested in rhymes than in the meaning of words, but even so, she was able to give some indication of the difficult times.

> He's give men job's
> Who were at the gate of death
> They were slowing dieing
> For the wan't of theft.[2]

In a later verse she expressed it even more graphically.

> People were dying
> And had nothing to eat
> Not even shoes,
> to wear on their feet[3]

For those who witnessed the depression there was much concern about the impact on the nation's political and social system. The alarm came from all elements of society. For example, a physician from Detroit tried to explain the situation to President Hoover in mid-1932. In a long poem he waxed somewhat philosophical, but three verses seem to express his concern for the future.

> Many people are forced into
> Losses, poverty, and sorrow
> And to hold to their belongings
> On credit they must borrow.

> After such extreme efforts
> Anxiously they watch it going
> They have not yet had a harvest
> Others reap what they were sowing.

> In this unbalanced situation
> Many must pay, The Few collect,
> Our country with its anxious people
> Is distressed and may be wrecked.[4]

Others were somewhat more angry. A woman from New York City wrote a poem with two parts—the first concerned the challenge of 1932 and the second dealt with the answer of 1934. Obviously, this was a tribute to Franklin D. Roosevelt, but the reader can see the anger in her mood. In 1932 she said:

We are the tillers and makers
    yet we starve midst the surplus of food
    we starve for the sake of the takers
    who slowly are drinking our blood.
    Arise then! Oh Voice! of our hunger!
    Swell out in a mighty hymn!
    We are the leaders and brothers
    of millions of hungry men....[5]

Roosevelt, she believed, had saved the people from dire calamity as a portion of the second part of the poem ("The Answer 1934") indicates.

We have a leader and thinker
    who saved us from losing our game
    when dispair and failure were threatening
    the growth of America's name
    when millions of people were starving
    though wheat bins were bursting with wheat
    in the grasp of the shirkers and takers
    who trampled our flag with their feet...[6]

Perhaps we had gone mad as a nation. Certainly a man from Akron, Ohio, thought so when he reflected upon conditions in 1935.

A Land of Beggars we've become
We have surely gone berserk,
The busiest place in town is the "Relief"
But yet there is no WORK.

Our Young they gad about the street
And truly nothing find to do.
And the folks that work ; Half time may find,
But that does not see them thru.

WE'VE RAISED THE PRICE OF HOGS AND WHEAT
AND DESTROYED THE PRODUCTS OF THE SOIL.
AND THE POOR CAN NO LONGER BUY THEM
FROM THE LITTLE INCOME OF THEIR TOIL.[7]

There were those who also saw in America's weakness signs of trouble for the whole world. Even though the 1930s was a time of isolationism in foreign policy many people still saw the United States as a world leader. One seventy-six-year-old gentleman from Cleveland, Ohio, tried to express this to President Hoover shortly before the election of 1932.

> Oh: America. Great America.
> A test of thy strength is begun.
> Shall thy mighty arm, thy vaunted power,
> Fade out like the setting sun?
> The eyes of the world are upon thee;
> From worried millions, in lands oer the sea.
> Oh: America, powerful America, what shall the answer be?[8]

This man was typical of a great many who wrote poetry to Hoover and Roosevelt in the 1930s. Older people had experienced depression before; they had lived through wars and political movements of various sorts. They were the one generation who had witnessed the transformation of the United States from an agrarian society to an industrialized giant. Most who expressed themselves indicated that they had not seen such extreme economic stress before. Some became bitter and disillusioned; others, such as the man from Cleveland, were still optimistic about the future. He had faith enough that he titled his poem, "The Answer." He told Hoover that he hoped that his efforts would "bolster up and maintain our faith which will ere long lead us out of our troubles."[9] The second verse of his poem expresses this feeling.

> Oh: America. Proud America.
> Gird on thy armor bright.
> Lead a floundering world thats discouraged and lost
> From darkness to safety and light.
> Raise aloft thy banner of trust and hope,
> That the uttermost world may see.
> Oh; America. God-fearing America.
> HAVE FAITH. Shall the answer be.[10]

Like many other depression poets, he was old and infirm. He apologized to Hoover for printing his letter, but he had no other choice since he was partially paralyzed.[11] Even so, he had not lost faith as his poem indicated.

Others who expressed optimism and hope also revealed conditions in their poetry. A young Texas girl expressed it this way.

The times are so hard
You can't even buy lard,
There's not enough money
And we can't buy honey.
It was 1931 and 1932
And I do hope it will soon be through,
We are all very sad
Why not cheer up and be glad.

The old men sit and gripe
When they should be cheery and bright,
The tramps walk the street
Asking for something to eat,
And seeking places to sleep.
We often hear
That better times are near,
So let's do our part
And give Roosevelt a start
And I do hope you are President.[12]

A woman from South Carolina, using a famous athlete of the day, said something about salaries and food.

If Ty Cobb would lend us his assistance,
In taking Old Depression for a ride,
In case Depression balked and showed resistance,
Ty could show him how to do that famous slide.
What he's done to our salaries is tragic,
He's played havoc with the workman's dinner pail,
We'll oust him if we have to use black magic,
In our lexicon there's no such word as fail.[13]

Despite the various poetic efforts a man from Kentucky pretty well summed up the entire situation. Even though his poem was long it deserves quotation in full because it was well written and covered just about every condition. He dedicated the poem to President Roosevelt in May 1933 when the famous "Hundred Days" was in progress and the hope of America had been raised by Roosevelt's dramatic actions.

When all the living world is bent and chaos bound,
When riot is unfurled and panic shakes the ground,

When factories idle stand and weeds grow in the yard,
When Hunger stalks the land with visage grim and hard.

When corn is fed to flames and wheat rots in the head,
When everything's to blame and confidence is dead.
When mine and shaft are closed and disease is in the camp,
When labor is deposed and poverty is ramp!

When tithes and taxes cost more than the land will make,
When cherished homes are lost in destitution's wake,
When money marts are dark and debts are long unpaid,
When merchants loss is stark and enterprise afraid.

When empty freighters ply across the seven seas,
When trade and commerce die for want of argosies,
When patriots in rags in vain appeal for aid,
When Socialistic hags the parliament upbraid.

When nations stand at arms with saber and with gun,
When direful alarms spread with each morning's sun,
When international greed has cast its spell of gloom,
When revolution's seed has bred the red commune.

When children cry for bread and drooping leave their play,
When toiling women dread the coming of each day,
When strong men find no task to feed their hungry brood,
When crime behind the mask assumes a violent mood.

When prophets false make bold sophistries to explore,
When vaults are piled with gold and starvation's at the door,
Lord, guide thy Captain's hand, give him but sight to see,
He'll steer the Ship of State through this tempestuous sea,
Lead Thou our hears aright from selfish paths we've trod,
Oh! Let Thy people see the light and the power of their God![14]

Specific areas of the economy suffered more than others, and some groups of people spoke up more often. Certainly one of the hardest-hit sectors of the economy was agriculture. Farmers had been suffering from economic depression since the end of World War I—a full ten years—before other segments of the economy began to feel the pinch. The unhappiness of the farmers was easy to understand.

In the poetry concerning farm conditions one finds very strong strains of the agrarian radicalism that motivated the leaders of the Populist movement more than thirty years before. Many of these were undoubtedly heir to the sentiments expressed by William Jennings Bryan in his "Cross of Gold" speech in 1896 when he said that farmers were the backbone of America and that the rest of the country—especially cities —had to recognize the importance of the farmer. In writing about the farmer some of the poets set these sentiments in rhyme.

One Californian was not modest in his description of agriculture as the key to all civilization.

> Hail to the Farmers who first built the Home,
> With Families as unit of the Clan,
> The Tribe, the State, the Nation and the Empires,
> Through all the Golden Ages of the world.
>
> Hail Agriculture then, and sing its Praise,
> As Founder of the Home and Family,
> The central arch of all Prosperity,
> The keystone to the Progress of Mankind.[15]

Even with all the trouble that agriculture had endured, its importance had not diminished as far as he was concerned.

> And Agriculture still remains the first,
> And supreme task of life, the bottom rock
> Sustaining all the rest. So it should be
> The first and chiefest care of Government,
> AS BASE OF ALL OUR CIVILIZATION.[16]

Evident in the poetry is the strong feeling that farmers should be revered for their contributions, but instead they were scorned and mistreated. Specifically the farmer had fed the world. A poem about the Farm Holiday movement quoted by two prominent agricultural historians attests to this.

> Come, fellow farmers, one and all--
> We've fed the world throughout the years
> And haven't made our salt.
>
> We've paid our taxes right and left
> Without the least objection

We've paid them to a government
That gives us no protection.[17]

In 1936 an Oklahoman said that the New Deal of Franklin Roosevelt recognized the farmer's contribution to society and would not desert them.

The farmer always fed the world,
He only asks his rights;
His products' prices now restored--
He's worked with all his might;
His family working in the field
To reap what he might sow;
Desert the man who feeds the world?
The NEW DEAL still says "NO".[18]

All sorts of problems existed. Many people could not understand the phenonomen of bumper crops that were virtually worthless on the market while hunger became more of a problem every day. This was already expressed in a poem previously quoted:

When millions of people were starving
though wheat bins were bursting with wheat[19]

Even though his grammar left something to be desired a resident of Pasadena, California, seemed incredulous when he asked

who ever seen a country with to much wheat
and so many people with nothing to eat.
nothing to eat and nothing to wear
heaps and heaps piled up every where.[20]

Not all farmers had crops they could not sell. Especially in the Great Plains the "dust bowl" days of the 1930s dashed the hopes of many who had been lured to the West by the potential high profits of another day. A freshman at the high school in Kim, Colorado, an area hard-hit by the drought, explained the dilemma of many farmers.

When we came out here to the golden west,
We rattled our money and felt the best.
Wheat and corn they both grew fine,
Pumpkin and squash grew large on the vine.

But at last here came the old sand storm;
It blew out our wheat, and ruined our corn.
The grass is covered up and the well went dry.
It killed our horses and our cows did die.

The machinery we bought and couldn't pay,
Then came the collectors and carried them away.
There's nothing left but grief and woe;
We can't stay here and we have no money to go.[21]

Cotton farmers were also badly hit by the depression. The situation got so bad that various political efforts were made to improve the lot of the cotton farmer. Huey Long, governor of Louisiana, even suggested a moratorium on cotton planting in 1932 in an effort to create a scarity that would drive prices up from the rock-bottom five cents per pound level to which they had fallen. Even though Long had a number of supporters, the plan was doomed.[22] The low price of cotton brought forth the efforts of some of the poets. One man, writing about conditions in Arkansas and the farmer's future, said conditions were bleak before the New Deal.

Cotton was cheap; in fact, 'way down,
Selling evewhere for a nickle a pound.

The farmer was working and breaking his back,
Picking <u>five-cent</u> cotton and dragging <u>a</u> sack.[23]

Five-cent cotton in Alabama also was responsible for two verses in a song that made the rounds in the South. The crudity of the song and the way it was sent to Roosevelt in no way imply that the sentiments were false. These were only two of seven verses from a Democratic campaign song in 1936.

With 5¢ Cotton How We gonna live, How
We gona How we gonna live
Down in Ala. Bam

5¢ cotton ant got no underware
got no underware, got no under
Ware. 5¢ Cotton underware
Down in Ala Bam.[24]

Obviously, farmers suffered severely during the depression. In fact, the conditions of rural life were a true tragedy. Some farmers, however, could still laugh and joke about their conditions despite the type of life they were forced to live. A good example was a farmer in Alabama who expressed it in the following way:

> My Mules Went lame in their hind feet.
> My Milk Cows They Went dry.
> The Moths eat up all my wheat and
> Then chewed up the rye.
> The Markets Went to less than Naught
> My Corn Brought less than Shucks
> And every thing I eat I bought on
> the credit then by Jucks.
> My only pair of home spun paints
> Wore Through before and after.
> And every time I'd back or advance I'd
> Catch cold In the drafter.
> My daughter ran off and married a
> Crook and came back with babe twins
> And now they're up running around
> Kicking me on my shins.[25]

Farmers as well as city dwellers contributed heavily to another tragic development of the Great Depression. As conditions worsened, unemployment in the cities grew to alarming proportions and more and more farmers found themselves driven off the land by consolidation and drought.

As these people looked for work, they moved from place to place. Sometimes the wanderers were men who had left their families at home while they searched in vain for that elusive job, but in many cases men on the move took their families with them. In other instances, many of those moving from place to place were young people out on their own, some of whom had left home to remove a burden from their families and others who were seeking work so that they could assist their families at home. There is no way to estimate the number of transients during the depression, but without doubt, it was large.

As the transients moved around the country, they aroused both the suspicion and sympathy of Americans who stayed at home. This homeless band of people also became the subject of some of the depression poetry.[26]

For example, one poet explained that the condition had existed for a long time. This was even more damnable since all the wanderers wanted was work.

> The unemployed have hunted work
> And yet he's walked the street--
> Since twenty nine he's been bowed down
> And asked that he might eat;[27]

Many people emphasized that these people were not asking for charity and were no threat to society. They were simply average people asking for a fair opportunity to make their own way by their own labor. As one songwriter from East St. Louis put it:

> Depressions got both you and me,
> And all are standing round,
> And every day we go and see
> If some work there may be found,
> No wonder some turn out so bad;
> Try and try, and all for nothing,
> But we'll fight and see what can be had,
> And hope that we find something.[28]

In the minds of the transients and those who observed them, the paradox of food surpluses and hunger side-by-side could not be explained. As one man exclaimed in the midst of a long poem:

> something to eat and something to wear
> for there's heaps and heaps, piled up every where.
> we are out of work our savings gone.
> now we'v joined that idle throng.[29]

Or as he said in another poem:

> Out of work not on the beat.
> how in the world can a poor man eat
> we walk the streets and see things so nice
> how in the world can we pay the price
>
> avlanche of butter and sugar and cant buy a lump
> cant see any way out to get over the hump.

> no bacon no beans and the cupboard bare
> not a scrapp of bread any where
>
> Too pround to begg to honest to steal
> have gone now weeks and weeks without square meal.
> an empty stumach and ragged pants
> who in the world has got a chance.
>
> our clothes wore out, our shoes run down.
> and old slouch hat with a hole in crown.
> tramping the streets our feet all sore
> dare not sit down, fear we cant rise no more.[30]

But the real dilemma was the condition in which they lived. In 1934 the gubernatorial election in California became news because of the candidacy of Upton Sinclair. Promoting a plan he called EPIC (End Poverty in California), Sinclair offered a threat to the power structure and frightened many people with his radical-sounding ideas. One of the campaign songs used in California was aimed at the transients who, the song said, would benefit from Sinclair's election. This group was a potential power group in California if it could be mobilized since California was the mecca for many of the uprooted described so well in John Steinbeck's *The Grapes of Wrath*. The first verse described something of the conditions of the transients.

> How many men are hungry away from family and home;
> Seeking a job they cannot find, From town to town they roam.
> How many homes are empty, The jobless pay no rent.
> Lacking shelter from cold or storm, not even a hut or tent.[31]

The second verse went on to explain that the EPIC plan, were it to be put into practice, would solve these problems.

As always, some of the poets described the conditions and tried to locate the blame. Often President Hoover was singled out as the villain as one woman from Arkansas explained:

> (3) There are men, women and
> children walking the roads
> and streets, begging for clothes
> and something to eat. The
> winter is here and the nights

are very cold and poor hungry
people are tramping in the
snow. Hoover in his mansion
with every thing so fair good
Things to eat, and plenty of
Clothes to wear, He is the
cause of many people being
out in the cold, with no
Place to call home nor no
where to go.[32]

Another person from California, despite his spelling and style, very adequately explained the dilemma from the transient's point of view.

I had to have work so I started out to look.
I searched th country over, and I looked in every nook
I walked,and walked, and walked,andthen I walked some more
I walked till my legs give out an till my feet were sore

I looked in all the papers and I chased all over town
I went to all the employment's offices every where around.
home I went at dark, and tumbled rite in bed.
and then to my troubled soul , a pain hitt me in the head.

Well I could not sleep, I tryed my very,very best
I rolled and tumbled all the night with out a bitt of rest.
I got up next morning feelding terrible sore,
to face the same old problems, just as the day before.

Yes the same old problems, and you know I was feelding blue.
there was no job in sight,and I did not know what to do
Bills were cuming in long past due, many were breathing
out slaughters and threats , saying what's the matter with you.[33]

Another man from Chicago who called himself "The Humanitarian Philosopher" wrote a poem in 1936 called "Do You Remember?" This was an effort to arouse support for Roosevelt in his first bid for re-election. Even though there were many people still wandering the country in 1936 there had been enough improvement to cause the poet to ask people if they remembered how bad things had been before Roosevelt became president.

There were millions upon millions
Whom, unenlisted, daily marched,
Sorely treading o'er rough lanes,
Hearts, nigh bitter--minds, ill-arched;

Young and old and halt, e'en infants
With dying mothers, all trod they
Seeking work for pauper's wages,
Or mere cot for tired head to lay;

Toilers, each. From 'shut-down' shop,
Idle mill, lost home, or farm,
Roved this "Army of Unemployed" victims,
Yet, no sought foes to bodily harm;

Did you see them dine on swill
To keep wed their body and soul?
Did you help enlarge the bread-lines
Where Death hid its "UNKNOWN" toll?

Were you among those made weakened
By oft' 'turn-down' at each chanced hope?
Were you amid those made foot-sore
Pursuing the vagabond's endless grope.[34]

Some of the most tragic cases were the young people on the road. A very good description of who these young people were and how they lived was provided in the midst of the depression by Thomas Minehan in a book he wrote from his experiences on the road with homeless children and young people.[35] One of the best descriptions of the problems faced by young people and the disillusionment they felt was provided by an amateur poet from Wisconsin.

We were the Legions of Unwanted Youth,
The Youth for whom the world could find no place;
We knocked long at opportunity's door;
It opened--to slam us in the face.

We wandered here and there--hither and yon,
Or sat and brooded silently at home,
For this was our choice--to eat the bread
From our hungry kin or aimlessly roam.

Days on the roads, nights in jungles and flops,
For young kids who should have been in schools.
Bread of idleness! Waters of discontent!
Our young hands asking for work and work's tools.

We wandered and brooded and tried to think;
Someway and somehow we'd get thru' the days.
It wasn't much wonder some of us slipped,
For this old world was one hell of a place.

Our youth and strength a drug on the market,
Nobody needed us! Nothing to do!
Unwanted youth! Eating unearned bread!
Maybe you think it's not hell to go thru'![36]

A problem of the depression which brought much emotion, and sometimes action, was the loss of property because of depressed conditions. The episodes in the Midwest where farms placed up for auction for non-payment of mortgages were purchased for a pittance after the officials were intimidated by local residents are well known. In some states, efforts were made for special legislation to prevent mortgage foreclosures because of the abnormal conditions.

Some of the poets mentioned the problems of eviction, but they were usually trying to soothe the feelings of those who were faced with this prospect. A high school student in Arizona said that all Americans had to do their share and to bear their own burdens, even

When your home is up for auction, and your jewelry's all in hock,
And you've used up every penny from the old proverbial sock,
   And your kids are going hungry, and their clothes are all in
   shreds,
And you've become the natural prey for communistic Reds;[37]

A man from Akron, Ohio, even sent Roosevelt his notice of eviction, but in the accompanying poem he was not bitter because he saw the action as a part of God's larger plan.

So what does it matter much
IF THEY DO PUT US IN THE STREET,
And we loose our LIFETIME CREDIT
Because our RENT WE CANNOT MEET.[38]

Another poet seemed to see this problem as something rather routine.

> Gas bill light bill and house rent due
> Hurry"Hurry" some wise man and tell us what to do.
> land-lord's at the door with stomping feet.
> says pays up old boy, er' ye go out in the street.[39]

Obviously, Americans had never faced anything like the depression. Various people reacted to it in many different ways, and these reactions will be discussed in more detail later. However, it seems appropriate to mention at this point that one woman believed that many people saw only one way out.

> (4) Such times has never
> Been till Hoover's
> Administration begin. Some
> Has been robbed, some has been
> mobbed, and some has gone insane.
> And thousands of others people
> Who lived all over the land
> Felt their troubles were so
> Great they thought they could
> not stand. They committed suicide
> and has gone to hell looking
> For a better place where their
> poor souls could dwell.[40]

If this woman was correct many people could not stand the strain and took the only way out they could find. She also lays the blame at the feet of Herbert Hoover. In this she was not alone. In fact, Americans seem to have a characteristic reaction to crisis. When things are bad, there seems to be a natural reaction to try to find someone or something to blame for the trouble. This was certainly the case during the depression.[41] Shortly after the depression began, the search for a villain occupied many people, including many of the poets.

# 4

# The Villain

In the midst of any crisis a tendency of human nature is to look for the cause of the problem and to lay the blame on some one individual. As so often happens the effort is made in wartime by those who oppose it to attach the responsibility upon one person. Because of the nature of our political system and its pervasive influence on American society the president in office usually receives the credit for good things and, more often, the blame for disasters. Historians are very familiar with the phrases: "Mr. Madison's War," "Mr. Lincoln's War," "Mr. Wilson's War," and "Johnson's War."

Whether the president in power is truly responsible for the success of certain policies or for the disastrous events that often overtake us really is irrelevant. As has been noted so often, perception is usually more important than reality. If the public perceives that Lyndon Johnson was responsible for Vietnam or that Richard Nixon planned and executed all the events associated with Watergate then there seems little to be gained in pointing out that there may have been others who were, in truth, responsible for certain events.

Another characteristic of our political system makes the perception even more important. As chief executive the president has often been compared to an elected king—especially in the twentieth century. With such a view of such a powerful office, the president becomes responsible for virtually everything that happens in American government. He bears the ultimate responsibility for all those subordinate to him regardless of their number or the varied levels of competency.

In many ways Herbert Hoover became a victim of the system. The Republican Party had claimed responsibility for the overall unprecedented prosperity of the 1920s; it was only logical for the public to hold the party responsible for the following collapse and debacle. As the head of the Republican Party Hoover felt the brunt of this shift in public opinion. Moreover, Hoover had been vaunted as the ultimate in leadership—the great engineer—in the election of 1928.

Therefore, since the depression became obvious during his presidential term and he seemed helpless to deal with it, the cause of the depression and its continuation was Herbert Hoover. Defenders of Hoover at the time and some historians in subsequent years tried to show that Hoover was not personally responsible, that he was, in fact, the victim of circumstances. Even so, the perception of a large portion of the American people was that Hoover *was* responsible. Thus, it was Hoover's depression.

Despite the tendency to blame Hoover, there were people who attributed the cause of the depression to other reasons. The search for a scapegoat began early and continued throughout the depression years, and beyond. The poets of the depression were as active as any in trying to find the cause.

The amateur poets, unlike other letter writers, seemed to concentrate on a few major causes. Others who tried to pin the blame for hard times looked for anything that might have had any responsibility for the debacle. One imminent historian of the era found almost all causes present in the minds of the general public:

> Opinions ranged from the highly sophisticated to the bizarre and ignorant. A few people even blamed the calamity on sun spots. Others said it was fate and dug into their copies of Nostradamus. Still others said the depression was the inevitable aftermath of the World War. A great many Puritan souls attributed the hardship to retribution for the good times of the 1920's and thought of the whole situation as a "hangover" or "the morning after." Marxists argued that the depression was inherent in the nature of capitalism and that the only cure was socialism. President Hoover believed that America's hardship was only a part of the general world malaise, that the United States had been dragged down by economic failure in Europe. From his point of view this was a comforting theory; it shifted the blame away from his administration and those of Harding and Coolidge and relieved American business leadership from the responsibility. . . . Hard-shell advocates of laissez faire blamed government "meddling." Their argument was that the Federal Reserve System's action in raising the rediscount rate in August 1929 had destroyed "confidence," one of their favorite words, in the stock market and had thereby precipitated the crash.[1]

A citizen writing to the leading newspaper in Texas listed almost all the same causes for the depression. He named almost all of them when he listed the following as causes of the depression: war debts, failure to join the League of Nations, a conflict between industrial and agricultural

America, the Federal Reserve System, speculation, the protective tariff, poor agricultural profits, and increased taxation.[2]

Despite these and other reasons people saw for the depression, the poets did not write about them very often. Some were mentioned, of course. High tariffs were mentioned by some as the cause of the trouble. In the middle of a long poem in 1938 from a Democratic Party leader in St. Paul, Minnesota, to Franklin D. Roosevelt that dealt with many issues, the tariff was mentioned. This was a poem addressed to Hoover.

> Thus millions were fooled,then came the crash;
> The people held the bag,your friends took the cash.
> The tariff racketeers were given their will
> When you signed the iniquitous Smoot-Hawley bill.
> Shops soon were closed,so were the mills,
> While your friends,the Capones,ran illicit stills.
> Trade was ruined,foreign markets disappeared
> When you darn idiots those tariff-walls reared.
> The country was afflicted with great tribulation
> When former customers countered with retaliation.[3]

Earlier during the presidential campaign of 1932, a high school teacher in California sent Hoover two poems written by students that had been published in the school paper. One of them dealt with the tariff, among other things.

> Our tariff's so high
>     That nothing comes in;
> Our poor foreign markets
>     Have shrunk till they're thin.[4]

Others believed the unemployment that caused the depression was the result of automation, a complaint heard since the beginning of the Industrial Revolution. A man from Newport, Kentucky, who was trying to console President Hoover, said it this way:

> It Is'nt Mr. Hoover's Fault
> Because You Can't Find Work,
> Tis The Men Who Invent The Machinery,
> Who Knock Thousands Out Of Work.[5]

Soon after the depression became serious and was acknowledged by most everyone, President Hoover urged people to have confidence.

Some people believed that alone would end the depression. After all, they said, it was caused because people were concerned enough after the stock market crash of 1929 that they quit spending money and deflation resulted. With consumer fear and reduced spending the economy went into a decline. Hoarding money as a hedge against hard times, a now-common practice, was a clear reflection of the fear stalking the nation. Therefore, the hoarders themselves were causing the depression. Thus these misers, themselves a cause of the depression, could end hard times by spending their money. A businessman from New York said it this way:

> In a country as united as our good,old U.S.A.
> Why don't you stop that worry,if depression comes our way?
> 'tis true money makes the mare go,but she wo'nt go very far,
> Without the brains of our countrymen,to be her guiding star,
> While money is a handly tool, 'tis dormant when alone,
> So dig into that deposit box and bank without a groan.
> Just let the brains of honest men,who have productive minds.
> Put hoarded monies back to work and U.S.A. will have good
>     times.
> . . . . . . . . . . . . . . . . . . . . . . . . . . . . . . . .
> Let's put our shoulder to the wheel of the schooner of the Nation.
> To shove and push her from the rut that's bothered all Creation.
> Some money now let's circulate 'twill help like thunderation,
> Unlock those greenbacks,which you hoard and bank within the
>     Nation.
> So be like those Colonials who surely carried through.
> Take that money out of hoarding.most any bank will do.
> Now all togather let's get set and give our all each day.
> For that's the way we'll pull her out of the rut in the U.S.A.[6]

   In the summer of 1932 a Republican leader from Salt Lake City sent Hoover a long poem attacking the Democrats as the Donkey. A portion of it concerned hoarders.

> No matter now where that poor Donkey went
> His heart was filled with a strange discontent
> For the voice of great Hoover through out all the land
> Had echoed and thundered, like some mighty band.
>
> He'd called on the cities to all do their bit
> To keep and to strengthen the old Red Cross kit.

And granaries emptied themselves at his might
And gold that was hoarded came back to the light.[7]

If hoarding were a cause of depression, it was really only the result of greed, an age-old human trait. People hoarded because they were afraid of the future.

For we are building immense structures
    And many Works of various kind
That Future Generations digging in the DUST of covered ages
    No doubt in surprise will surely find,

And all this is happening in a NATION
That is the Wealthiest in the World
But we fear that the GOLDEN CALF we WORSHIP
Will soon be ground to powder, and into the pit be hurled[8]

Whatever some people believed, it was just greed according to a woman from New Hampshire who told Hoover:

Again things have come to a pretty pass
The same old hate and greed
The same old lust for fame and power
Still lives in Adam's seed.[9]

If all this hoarding had started with the stock market crash and if greed caused people to try to get rich quick and easy, then some people were convinced that the real villain had to be Wall Street and those who encouraged speculation in the stock market. The fear and hatred of Wall Street was nothing new. The Populists of the 1880s and 1890s had targeted Wall Street as the primary enemy. During the depression an old Populist from Texas, "Cyclone" Davis, still believed Wall Street was the cause of all evil.

The Wall Street bandits
In their lust
Have trampled the people
Into the dust.

They have robbed millions
Of all their feed

In order to gorge
Their sordid greed.

They have robbed the populace
Of their home
And put them out
On the earth to roam.

They have gathered wealth
In great big stacks
And piled up debts
On the peoples backs.

In this grand style
They live at ease
They fear no law
As do as they please

And the man who robs a country bank
He only robs by retail
These bandits who in millions rank
Rob by slaughter wholesale.

If hailed into court
By the powers that be
Most of our courts
Just set them free.[10]

The criticism of Wall Street was pointed. A woman from Vicksburg, Mississippi, minced no words.

Hoover blew the whistle:
Mellon rang the bell;
Wall Street gave the order,
and the country went to --[11]

A salesman from Chicago in a long poem to Roosevelt in 1938 called "Man Made Recession" found many causes for the depression. His attacks were aimed mostly at the rich and big business, but the stock market leaders and speculators came in for most of his wrath as these selected verses show.

That "Hell's broke loose" you'll all agree
But what's the cause will you tell me;
Some say its taxes, labor laws,
The fight on business is the cause.

Some say that merchants over-stocked,
That financiers the boat have rocked;
Big business on a sit-down strike,
All pay-roll fillers in dislike.

Some blame it on our politics,
Those wild jackasses from the sticks;
Some say that Roosevelt's to blame,
And tack "Recession" to his name.
. . . . . . . . . . . . . . . . . . . .
They rigged the market plenty high,
You'd think the limit was the sky;
Then all the "Big Shots" in the know,
Sold out fast and got their "dough."

The bubble burst, the market broke;
To millions it was not a joke;
'Twas surely not a "One-way ride"!
"Big Business" soon would stem the tide![12]

After Roosevelt became president one of the first acts of the New Deal was to pass the Securities and Exchange Act that established the Securities and Exchange Commission (SEC) to regulate stock trading. This was a popular measure, partly because of the distress caused by the collapse of the speculative bull market in 1929 and the belief of many that stock traders were dishonest.

The reaction of the poets in the aftermath reflected both their feelings about the stock market before regulation and their support for the SEC. In a poem from a man in Maine that defended Roosevelt's actions, he put words in the president's mouth.

Now when they withdraw they will find it all there,
But before often found that the 'cupboard was bare.'
I put a curb on the 'boys' running Wall Street, you know
Before this they sure took the Public in tow.
They'd sell folks 'securities' Sir 'till it hurt,
And when they'd come to - they'd be minus their shirt.

And you'd find that no matter what stocks you went inter
That the 'Boys' had gone South with your funds for the winter.
Now you don't get the interest you did on your funds,
But the Principal's there, when you die, for your sons.[13]

A person from Oklahoma City said in 1936 that the changes brought
to the stock market should be maintained so that it could not wreak
havoc again.

Shall we return to graft and greed,
Back to that weary street?
That street from which we have emerged,
From fear, shall we retreat?
Back to that dreary street of war,
Autocracy and woe?
Shall we turn backward in this fight?
The NEW DEAL still says "NO".[14]

As was true in so many ways, the president in office bears the brunt
of public opinion. A Texas woman tried to console Hoover while he was
still in office and said he was not responsible for the stock market crash.
The poem was addressed to people who were criticizing Hoover.

You were weak enough to buy,
"Worthless tocks" from some fall guy,
You lose your "Jack" you cry and cry,
    you're to blame-
not Mr. Hoover![15]

Later in 1938 criticism of President Roosevelt was mounting on
many fronts. A judge in New York City wrote a poem to cheer him up
and to counter the critics. One verse dealt with the brokers and bankers.

Just go down to Broad and Wall,
And blow a bugle call!
All hands turn out, giving the "Roosevelt Squawk."
Bankers fat and brokers lean
Will apear upon the scene;
You'll hear them shout,
Giving the "Roosevelt Squawk,"
Squawking about their taxes,
Sharpening up their axes,

Sobbing about the S.E.C., N.L.R.B. and O.G.D.,
"Business isn't worth a damn,"
Bulls and bears can't trim a lamb;
Just hear them all, giving the "Roosevelt Squawk."[16]

Businessmen, whether they were bankers, stockbrokers, or indus-
trialists, came in for their share of criticism for causing the depression.
The age-old tension between those who controlled jobs and the economy
and those who worked or were otherwise controlled or influenced by
business became pronounced again during the 1930s. Many people
believed after hard times came that Hoover, the man they had thought
was a humanitarian, was more interested in the welfare of business than
he was in the average person. A man from Oak Park, Illinois, said it this
way:

When in despair the nation lay,
With hunger stalking at the door
The desperate mob were kept at bay
By promises and nothing more.

Impotent sat the Nation's chief
Pledged to act as he was told,
Holding for the rich a brief,
To the rest his heart was cold.[17]

"Big Business" became a derogatory term to many. For them, these
men were greedy and selfish. They looked out for their own interests and
controlled government to achieve their goals. According to Cyclone
Davis, an old Texas Populist, corporate leaders were too disreputable to
be tolerated.

When truth lies down forever crushed,
And freedom's voice in fear is hushed,
And the toiling man is made a slave,
To add to the wealth of a corporate knave.[18]

For some the business leaders could not be trusted. They exploited
the people and then asked for help when times got bad because they
claimed they were the only ones who could restore prosperity. They
tended to ignore that they may have been a contributing factor in causing
hard times. A man from Baltimore did not accept the argument of
businessmen.

At one time the states had the power of interstate regulation,
So they proceeded to enact control legislation.
The result was, as unwritten history relates,
Then corporate interest proceeded to regulate the states.

They object to stocks and bonds being subjected to official
    investigation,
And affirm all such laws are vicious legislation.
They say all bankers and brokers should be trusted
Until they have skimmed the cream and left us busted.[19]

Another man seemed to doubt that business could be trusted.

Oh, big capital you know what to do?
In the world there's lots of trouble,
   this trouble is from you,
We see Depression does not go,
Give us work, let it be so,
Depression, Depression no more.[20]

To a man in Mississippi, Henry Ford seemed to epitomize the power of big business.

With rattling carloads of cheap tin,
    Ford has amassed and hoarded gold;
And now, to climax this great sin,
    Employees votes he dares control.[21]

For many who watched public affairs, business seemed to be favored over everyone else. In the aftermath of the veterans' bonus march expulsion from Washington by military force, a man from Minnesota said what many others probably believed.

Two million dough-boys cannot have their dough
It's all been "doled" to millionaires to make their steam yachts go.
Baa Baa Black Republican, have you any yen,
Millions, for millionaires, but not for jobless men.
Doles for Big Business, none for the small
That's the way that Hoover brings Prosperity to all.[22]

Foreign interests were also benefited over Americans, some believed. A poem in a Chicago magazine supposedly was written by a former

Industrial Workers of the World (IWW) leader who had served a prison sentence after World War I for radical activity. Even so, his sentiments probably reflect the thoughts of many who would not have considered themselves radical.

> Don't talk to us of "confidence,"
>     Our faith has been destroyed.
> You've proved that words can never feed
>     Twelve millions unemployed.
> You helped the foreign Money Kings--
>     The banks and railroads, too,
> They love you, Mr. Hoover,
>     But we've had enough of you.[23]

Business could lead during prosperity, some said, but the leaders became weak and ineffective when their practices led to trouble. Business really did not care about the people, but it could not cope with the consequences of its own actions.

> Alas! "Big Business," timid souls,
> Just slunk away like midnight ghouls;
> For capital's timid, turns real pale,
> When human rights are on the scale.
>
> All business reeled throughout the land,
> Fear, want, then followed hand in hand;
> Brave Hoover tried to cheer the mob
> 'Till Rosevelt assumed the job.[24]

Businessmen ran the country, some believed, but when their leadership failed, they came running to the government for help. At the beginning of Roosevelt's administration banking was on the verge of collapse. The first act of the new president was to issue an executive order closing all banks. A woman from Idaho thought the bankers were ungrateful for the help they received.

> IN THE YEAR NINETEEN HUNDRED THIRTY TWO
> BANKERS KNEW NOT WHAT TO DO
> TO THE GOVERNMENT THEY DID RAIL
> "SAVE US ELSE WE ALL FAIL."

THE PRESIDENT LISTENED TO THEIR PLEA
THEN INITIATED THE BANK GUARANTEE
BANKS DEPOSITS THEN NEARLY DOUBLED
BANKERS ARE NO LONGER TROUBLED.

AFTER THEIR SHARE OF GOVERNMENT MONEY HOGGING
THEY ALL SAY OTHER ADVANCES IS BOONDOGLING
THE GOVERNMENT NOW SHOULD NOT LEND
ITS HARD TO FIGURE THE BANKERS TREND.[25]

President Hoover and the Republican Party were considered by more people the cause of the depression than anything else. The attacks came mostly from Democrats who believed that twelve years of Republican control of the government had set the policies in place that caused such suffering by the 1930s. Many Democrats who abandoned their traditional party in 1928 to vote for Hoover over Al Smith felt themselves betrayed by the depression, which they laid at the feet of Hoover and the Republican Party.

Attacks on Republicans often included President Hoover and other Republican office holders. Andrew Mellon, secretary of the treasury and a prominent millionaire, often appeared in poetry. Occasionally Oscar DePriest, an African American Republican congressman, sometimes appeared as well, especially if the poet were a Southerner. A man from Reidsville, North Carolina, mentioned them both. This is part of a poem he sent to Roosevelt during the campaign of 1932 when FDR was scheduled to appear in Raleigh, North Carolina. In his cover letter he said, "I regret I can't come to Raleigh but it's too far to drive a 'Hoover cart.' I have neither gas nor car."

In nineteen hundred and twenty-eight,
    We recall it, time and again,
Millions of voters rushed the gates,
    To catch Prosperity's train.

With Herbert Hoover as their engineer,
    They were told to have no fears;
The tickets were good, the track was clear,
    Four four more prosperous years.
. . . . . . . . . . . . . . . . . . . .
Millions of voters since that disaster,
    Haven't cleared a single dime;

And though that train is puffing faster,
I'm sure they won't forget the time.

Herbert Hoover blew the whistle,
And DePriest rang the bell,
A. Mellon shouted, "All Aboard!"
And business went to Hell.[26]

Hoover was mentioned often, of course, since he was the most prominent Republican. A woman from Kentucky said that Hoover and the Republicans had failed the test.

Poor Hoover has had an acid test,
Now, we think he needs some rest,
Altho, we know he's done his best,
Republicans have had their way,
Let's give the democrats their day,
And when they get there let them stay.[27]

A Texan believed also that the Republicans were not equal to the task they faced. They had twelve years, but by 1932 they did not know what to do. These two verses are from a longer poem in which the poet attempted to use African American dialect for a humorous effect.

Republicans have had their chance,
And failed at the art of finance,
They've failed to hit,
And will have to admit,
That wid us, they've tore their pants.

If we had what we haven't got,
We certainly would have a lot,
The Republicans stroke,
Has got us all broke,
So let us try to change the plot.[28]

This theme was used by a West Virginian who believed that Republicans could no longer be trusted. Woodrow Wilson, the last Democratic president, had the country in good shape, but then Republicans took power and problems came. One might argue that the poet was wrong about depression coming immediately, but no one can mistake his point of view.

TWELVE YEARS.has the old wheels,been standing
and never,have they rolled around
when WILSON.walked out from the WHITE HOUSE
the wheels,of INDUSTRY.slowed down

WE know the old wheels,of INDUSTRY
are all rusty, from standing so long
but ROOSEVELT.has OIL.that will start them
to rolling so gently along[29]

A man from Michigan had the same sentiments, but he seems to have had a better grasp on the timing of the beginning of hard times.

Three long years - three loonngg years
First there was thirty and then thirty-one
Thirty-two followed but nothing was done
The Republican Party just clouded the sun
For three long years.

They closed all the factories and boarded them neat
They turned all the workers out into the street
If you did'nt have dividends you could'nt eat
For three long years.

Their ears were attuned to Prosperity's call
The farmer got nothing in spring or in fall
The poor stricken banker really needed it all
For three long years.[30]

As the presidential election of 1936 approached, other Republicans, especially those who might be the Republican nominee, came in for their share of blame. Many people who sent poems to Roosevelt assumed that whoever the nominee might be would be only another Republican who could do no better than Hoover and would attempt to reinstate Republican policies that had caused the problem in the first place. As Alfred Landon of Kansas became the obvious Republican leader, the amateur poets aimed their guns at him. A woman from Alabama sent Roosevelt a long handwritten poem soon after the election was over. Different parts of the poem are confusing since some verses assume Landon has won and others talk about how bad things will be if he is elected. It is probably safe to assume that the poet occasionally wrote from the perspective of how people would feel if Landon won. Selected verses reflect this woman's concern.

>Now I got Clothes, Now I got shoes
>I an't got no Hard time Blues.
>But if Landon gets in our pocket Book will Close
>So we Can't sleep not even dose.

>When Republicans Were in they done as they please
>But we ate lard Gravy and them old Cow peas.
>I ate them things till my stomach was afright
>I almost vomitt at every Bite.
>. . . . . . . . . . . . . . . .
>When Landon gets in the White house
>he will live just swell,
>he'll draw his pay not work a day
>And the rest can go to hell.

>We will sell our eggs for 1/2 cent
>Our cotton it wont sell.
>With Landon in the White house
>I'll tell you its worse than hell.[31]

During the campaign of 1936 a man from Kalamazoo, Michigan, sent Roosevelt a campaign song set to the tune of "Oh, Susanna" that expressed a similar opinion of Landon and the Republican Party.

>I've been reading all your speeches
>And to me they're "so much rot,"
>You're just like old man Hoover
>With his "chicken in each pot".
>That Republican baloney
>That they've fed the folks for years
>Has grown so stale, we're all fed up,
>I'm glad we are-----THREE CHEERS!

>Oh, Alf Landon, let's cut out all hot air,
>Let's meet each issue face to face and keep it on the square.[32]

By far, most of the blame was placed directly on Herbert Hoover. To many, his policies were heartless and were planned to impoverish the American people. Others who did not believe him to be an evil man did blame him for being naive or weak or badly advised. The criticism of Hoover was so widespread and the poems were so numerous that only a small sampling can be presented here.

Soon after the stock market crash of 1929 signalled the beginning of hard times, the poetic attacks on Hoover began. As things got worse the criticism intensified. By the time of the election of 1932 the attacks were greater. One approach was to blame Hoover directly and personally for causing the depression. Some of the poets seemed to think Hoover deliberately wanted people to suffer while others considered him merely inept or led by other unscrupulous persons. Many of the attacks on Hoover for causing the depression were presented in the form of Democratic campaign songs, slogans, or poems. For example, a man from Colorado Springs, Colorado, made it clear who was responsible.

> All should thank Franklin Roosevelt,
> And that is not a guess,
> No apologies to Hoover,
> Who got us in the mess.[33]

During the summer of 1932 a man from Globe, Arizona, who called himself "one of the ten million idle during the great Hoover's administration" sent a poem to candidate Roosevelt in which he questioned Hoover's motives. He wondered if Hoover were being cynical as he sought reelection in 1932.

> President Hoover must admit,
>     And with frankness confess,
> His tenure in office,
>     Brought us grief and distress.
> Why encourage us now
>     "say" the times are better
> When we borrowed three cents,
>     For a stamp on this letter.
>
> To let a nation suffer
>     three years; then say "now'"
> Just before the election
>     We,ll prove to the voter how'
> We can bring back prosperity.
>     Why has he waited so long?
> Made us a nation of beggars
>     Of about ten million strong.

The question what he,ll do,
    Will be meted by what he has done?
Have we enjoyed any prosperity
    Since his term of office begun?
If just before the election
    He knows how to restore
The prosperity of the nation
    Why not have done it before.

. . . . . . . . . . . . . . . . . .

He boasts of our wealth,
    Its a delusion and sham,
When the worth-while citizen,
    Can,t earn bacon or ham.
But why discuss the subject
    As to his ability or worth,
When in three years we,ve been reduced
    To the most poverty stricken nation on earth.[34]

Some called Hoover's reputed skills into question as in the case of a man from Idaho.

Herbert Hoover won the race,
In Nineteen Twenty-eight,
Solemn financier he was,
Who said he could dictate,
How to run America—
But not into the muck,
And now when we are all dead broke
He says its just "hard luck"![35]

Others, such as the woman from Fort Worth, Texas, thought Hoover had to be acknowledged.

O Roosevelt! O Roosevelt!
Canst thou deliver me
From all the things on this old earth
By Hoover caused to be?[36]

Two other Texans resorted to gimmicks during the campaign to show the contrast between the candidate and to pin the depression on Hoover.

NO MORE

H oover    a
                n
   unger      d

with

C urtis    a
             n
   confussion   d

WE WANT

R oosevelt   a
               n
   efreshment  d

with

G arner   a
            n
   roceries   d[37]

R oosevelt
   epeal
   eligious freedom
   eal Americanism

H oover
   ard Times
   unger
   itch hiking
   uman bug
   ell[38]

The people had been fooled long enough, said another Texan.

   You cannot fool, said Honest Abe
   All of them all the time
   And while musing that great man's sayings
   I have written this humble rhyme

For as one of the fooled and forgotten
Who has finally seen the light
I am convinced that Hoover had rather
Be President than right.[39]

Still another Texan agreed that change was necessary.

There's a long, long rest awaiting for Herbert Hoover, we know,
He has made an awful mess of things as manager of the show.
For the past three years he's straddled all of the fences in the land-
and now we crave the frankness of Roosevelt—he's the man.[40]

Even after Hoover's defeat in 1932, some Democrats did not let up on him. They continued to send poetry to Roosevelt reminding him how bad Hoover had been and how he had caused hard times. A portion of a thirteen-page poem from a man in Long Beach, California, made it clear that the country did not want Hoover back.

Like a drowning man grasps a straw,
    to swim or sink
We don't want things back
    where they were four years ago
Before Roosevelt came to help us,
    it was a sorry show
Even the Indians refused to take,
    the country back again.[41]

A freshman at Reed College in Oregon told Roosevelt that Hoover had caused the problems and yet he dared to criticize Roosevelt.

We gave him a chance
And he ran things wrong
And brought us into where we are,
And now he jigs and shrieks his song,
And says the President's gone "too far".[42]

An Ohio resident said that Hoover might want to get back into office but he had been outsmarted.

NOW HERBERT HOOVER AND OTHERS LIKE HIM ALL,
ARE PLANNING FDR'S DEFEAT NEXT FALL,

RECOV'RY ALL OF THEM HAVE TRIED TO STALL,
BUT THEY HAVE BEEN OUTSMARTED.[43]

The country was better off without his leadership, according to a man from New Jersey.

Lets not overlook friend Herbert.
A glorified Chief Clerk.
He abolished poverty for the rich
But his two-chicken gag didn't work.

Yes, Herbie is quite a fella.
He wisecracks now like sin.
He tells us how but we all know
That he's better Out than In.[44]

Part of the criticism of Hoover was directed at him because he and his supporters had made a big issue of the "Republican prosperity" of the 1920s and pledged its continuation during his administration. Hoover had the misfortune of facing the stock market crash within seven months of taking office. Most of his term was consumed with trying to cope with the worsening economic condition. In that situation the promises of the Republicans to continue prosperity were impossible to keep. One of the campaign songs sent to Hoover that made such promises said it well.

Who's the man they choose to run from Key West to Vancouver,
He's the best of all the rest his name is Herbert Hoover;
With him keep prosperity, In this land of liberty,
After all is said and done, He's the man for Washington.

He's the right man to succeed our president Cal Coolidge,
Hoover's an executive and has tremendous knowledge;
Presidents Republican, have brought progress to our land,
If good times you wish to see, Line up with the G.O.P.[45]

Many Republicans in 1928 emphasized the role Hoover had played in the aftermath of World War I when he was appointed European relief administrator by President Woodrow Wilson. Hoover did an outstanding job in feeding the hungry of Europe and saving them from starvation. He became known as a great humanitarian and much was made of it in 1928. One campaign song said:

When the people cried for bread,
When rebuffs they got instead,
When they suffered cold and hunger
And couldn't stand it any longer. . . .,
    Who got for the starving food?
    Who found for the freezing wood?—HOOVER!
. . . . . . . . . . . . . . . . . . . . . . . . . .
When the East had no more food,
When their people were naked, nude,
When the world was weeping, crying
And mankind was starving, dying. . . .
    Who all of himself to others gave?
    Who saved millions from the grave?—HOOVER![46]

These sentiments were countered by Hoover's opponents during the election of 1932. For example, a man in Minnesota said it this way:

You said you'ld cure us of what ails,
You promised us full dinner pails,
Moster Hoover, When do we eat?
Prosperity's around the corner,
We're sucking thumbs like Jackie Horner,
Mister Hoover, When do we eat?
Don't blame us for being doubting Thomases,
For we can't live on idle promises.
You saved Germany, so they say,
Now save the "Good Old U.S.A."
Mister Hoover, When do we eat?[47]

Despite the attacks, Hoover did have his defenders, but they were not as numerous after 1929 as they had been before. The poems seemed to follow a similar theme. For example, two women from St. Joseph, Missouri, tried to console Hoover after his defeat in 1932.

Depression's been fought
From dawn until day.
The unfortunate cared for
All will say.
The path is now cleared,
The follower can see.[48]

A man from Kentucky believed Hoover had the country on the right track but was prevented from carrying his program to completion.

> You had the country on the mend
> Had this depression near an end
> Had business on the upward trend
> By sane and normal methods when
> Franklin D. Roosevelt stepped in
> With his alphabetical brain trusters
> pledge breakers and promise busters.[49]

Many other causes for the depression were suggested by people across the country. Although poets dealt with various causes of trouble, they were not as prolific on this subject as they were on many other topics. They blamed Hoover, Republicans, big business, and the rich. Most of the poets concentrated on other subjects such as the various New Deal agencies, but before that happened Roosevelt had to be elected. As the depression reached its low point in 1932 many of the poets began to see rays of hope. One of the greatest hopes, of course, was Franklin D. Roosevelt.

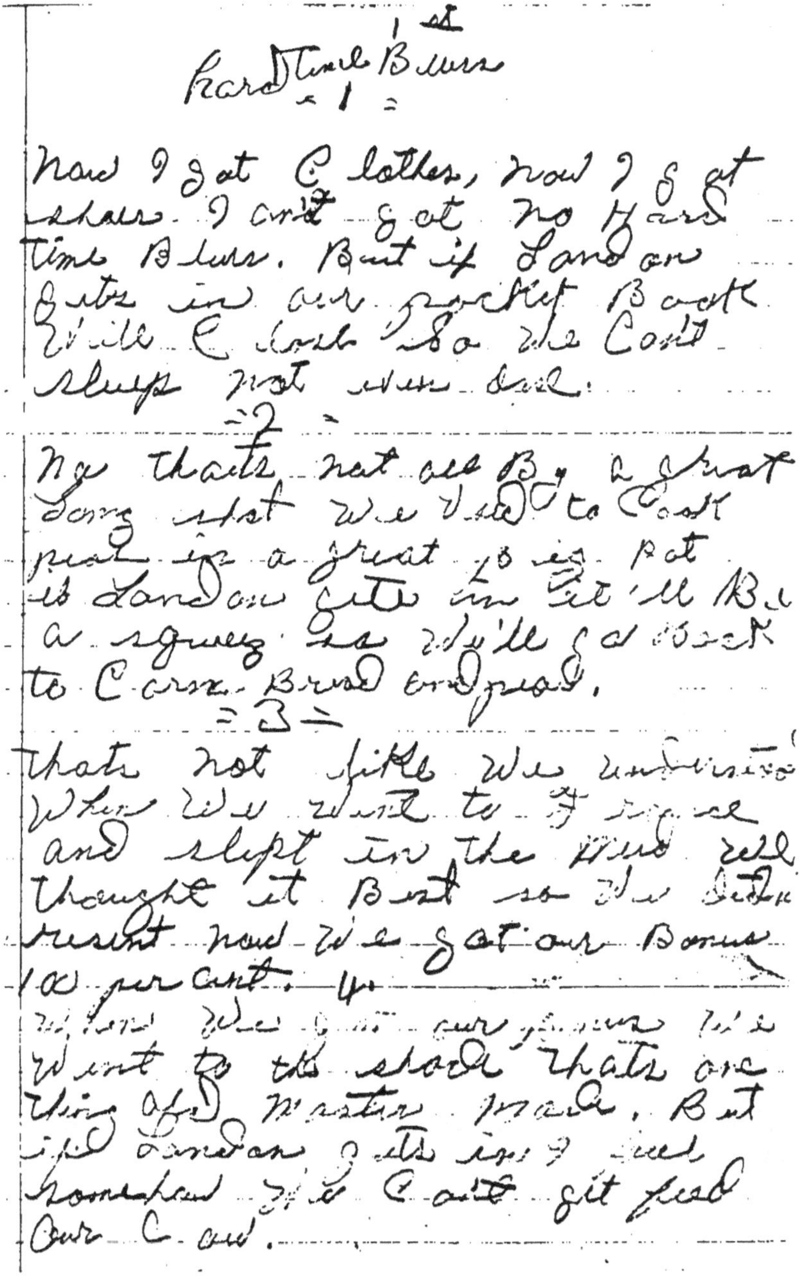

Fig. 1. Typical poem in the Roosevelt collection. Credit: Franklin D. Roosevelt Library.

# The Standard Bearer
(Dedicated to Franklin D. Roosevelt)

— · — ○ — · —

Thou bearer of a deathless name,
Proud heritage of worth and fame,
    To thee, All Hail!
Thou goest forth, like knight of old,
With burnished shield and heart of gold,
    Thou canst not fail!

With armor girded for the fight
For sacred liberty and right,
    Thou wilt not quail!
Fling forth thy banner to the sky,
Mankind and justice sanctify,
    Thou must prevail!

We come, we come, with gladsome cry
All greed and evil to defy,
    A vast host we!
A Roosevelt leads the mighty throng
To give us justice, undo wrong,
    On to victory!

Fig. 2. Typical poem in the Roosevelt collection. Credit: Franklin D. Roosevelt Library.

IF:

All night long you lie awake;
With a nasty, gripin' tummy ache;
Doctor's pills you refuse t  take,
    you're to blame-
not Mr. Hoover!

You awake too late to bathe and eat;
Off you go, rarein' down the street;
Car is crowded, there's no seat,
The wild crowd knocks you off your feet,
    you're to blame-
not Mr. Hoover!

You've loads and loads of work to do,
You stall and stall the whole day through;
The big boss shouts: " Overtime you'll do! "
    you're to blame-
not Mr. Hoover!

You were weak enough to buy,
"Worthless tocks" from some fall guy,
You lose your "Jack" you cry and cry,
    you're to blame-
not Mr. Hoover!

During nineteen thirty-two
You meet a girl of twenty-two;
Your family changes from one to two,
    you're to blame-
not Mr. Hoover!

IF, later, you need to buy
a go-cart for a tiny guy;
It'll do no good for you to sigh, cause,
    you're to blame-
not Mr. Hoover!

Some folks don't like my style, I'll vow,
But it's too late to change it now;
If things don't change this fall, don't me-o-o· o-o-w,
    you'll be to blame-
not Mr. Hoover!

Fig. 3. Typical poem in the Roosevelt collection. Credit: Franklin D. Roosevelt
Library.

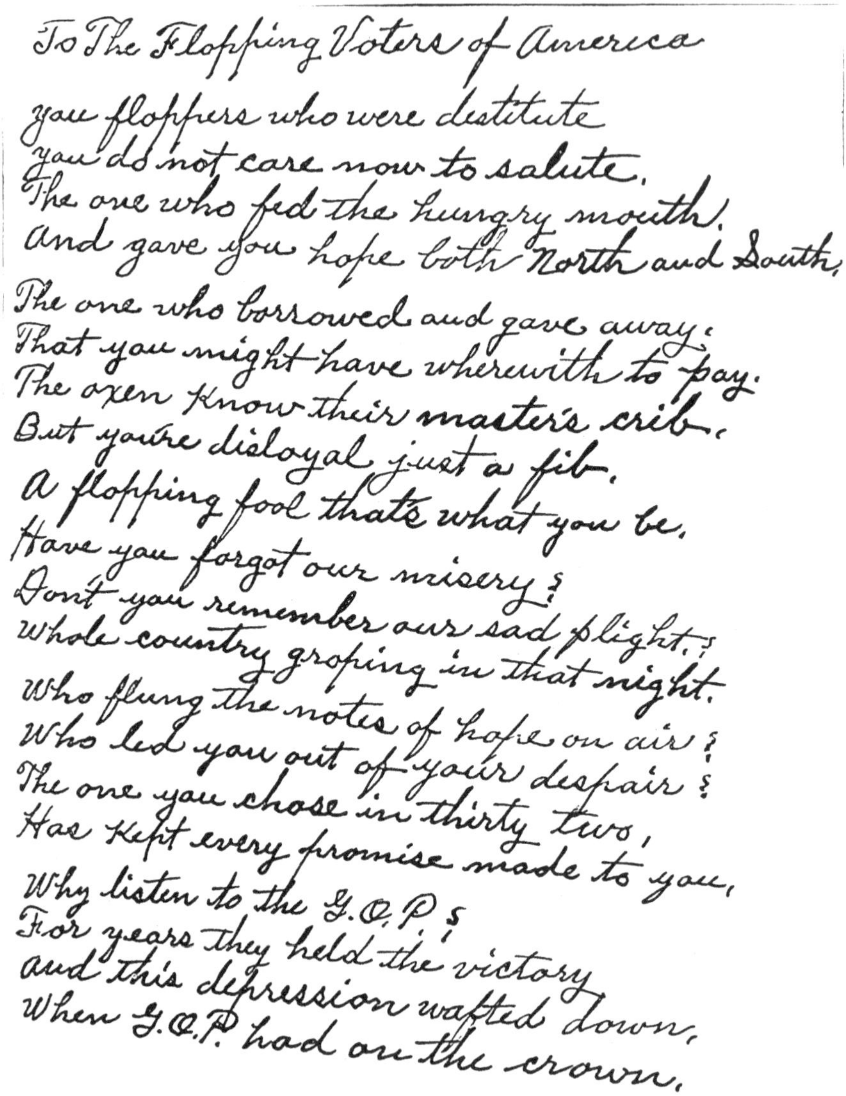

To The Flopping Voters of America

You floppers who were destitute
You do not care now to salute.
The one who fed the hungry mouth,
And gave you hope both North and South,
The one who borrowed and gave away.
That you might have wherewith to pay.
The oxen know their master's crib.
But you're disloyal just a fib.
A flopping fool thats what you be,
Have you forgot our misery?
Don't you remember our sad plight,
Whole country groping in that night.
Who flung the notes of hope on air?
Who led you out of your despair?
The one you chose in thirty two,
Has kept every promise made to you,
Why listen to the G. O. P.?
For years they held the victory
And this depression wafted down,
When G. O. P. had on the crown.

Fig. 4. Typical poem in the Roosevelt collection. Credit: Franklin D. Roosevelt
Library.

Fig. 5. Promotional poster for the Civilian Conservation Corps. Credit: Franklin D. Roosevelt Library.

Fig. 6. The third term issue was a favorite subject of the editorial cartoonists. Credit: *Washington News* from Franklin D. Roosevelt Library.

Fig. 7. The proposed changes in the Supreme Court brought vigorous reaction.
Credit: *Washington Star* from Franklin D. Roosevelt Library.

Fig. 8. Mrs. Roosevelt did not escape the cartoonists, especially with her travels. Credit: *San Francisco News* from Franklin D. Roosevelt Library.

CHRISTMAS EVE PREPARATION.

Fig. 9. An apparently confident Roosevelt was anxious to take over Hoover's job. Credit: *Washington Star* from Franklin D. Roosevelt Library.

Fig. 10. During World War II Roosevelt relaxed as he watched training maneuvers. Credit: Franklin D. Roosevelt Library.

Fig. 11. Civilian Conservation Corps members at work on the fire line in a forest. Credit: Franklin D. Roosevelt Library.

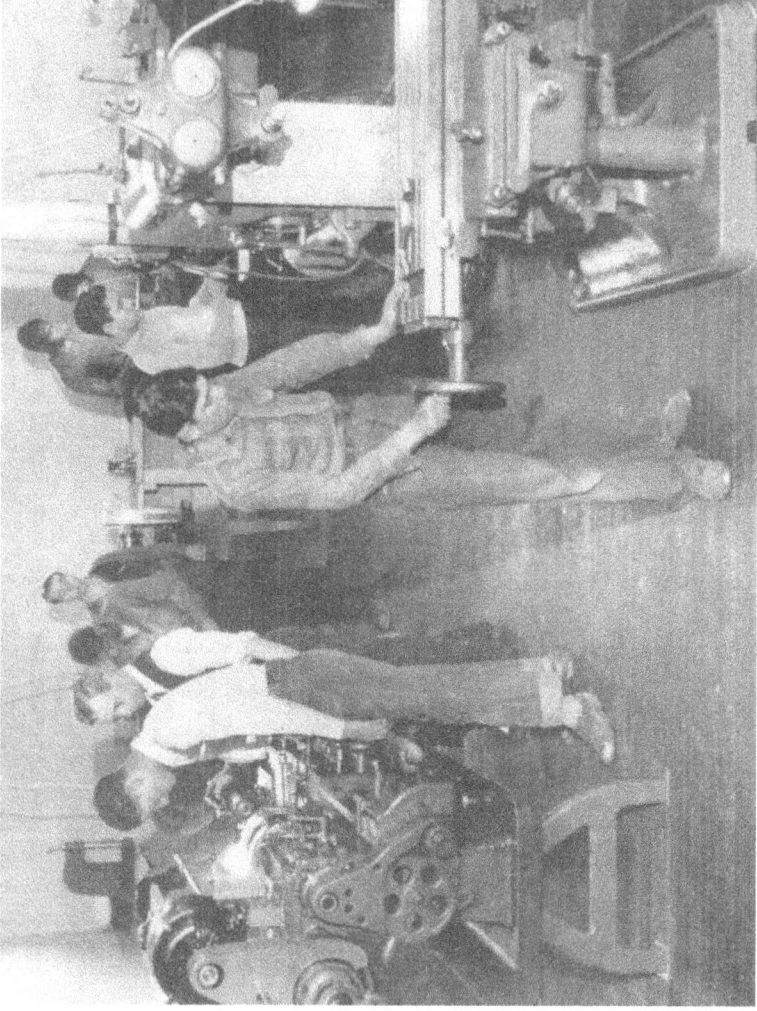

Fig. 12. The National Youth Administration provided jobs in an effort to keep young people in school, as in this machine shop in Chicago Heights. Credit: Franklin D. Roosevelt Library.

Fig. 13. The National Recovery Administration was one of the most widely publicized programs of the New Deal. Credit: Franklin D. Roosevelt Library.

Fig. 14. Breadlines became an all too common sight in America during the 1930s. Credit: Franklin D. Roosevelt Library.

Fig. 15. The Works Progress Administration provided jobs and did essential work, as cleaning up after a flood in Louisville, Kentucky, in 1937. Credit: Franklin D. Roosevelt Library.

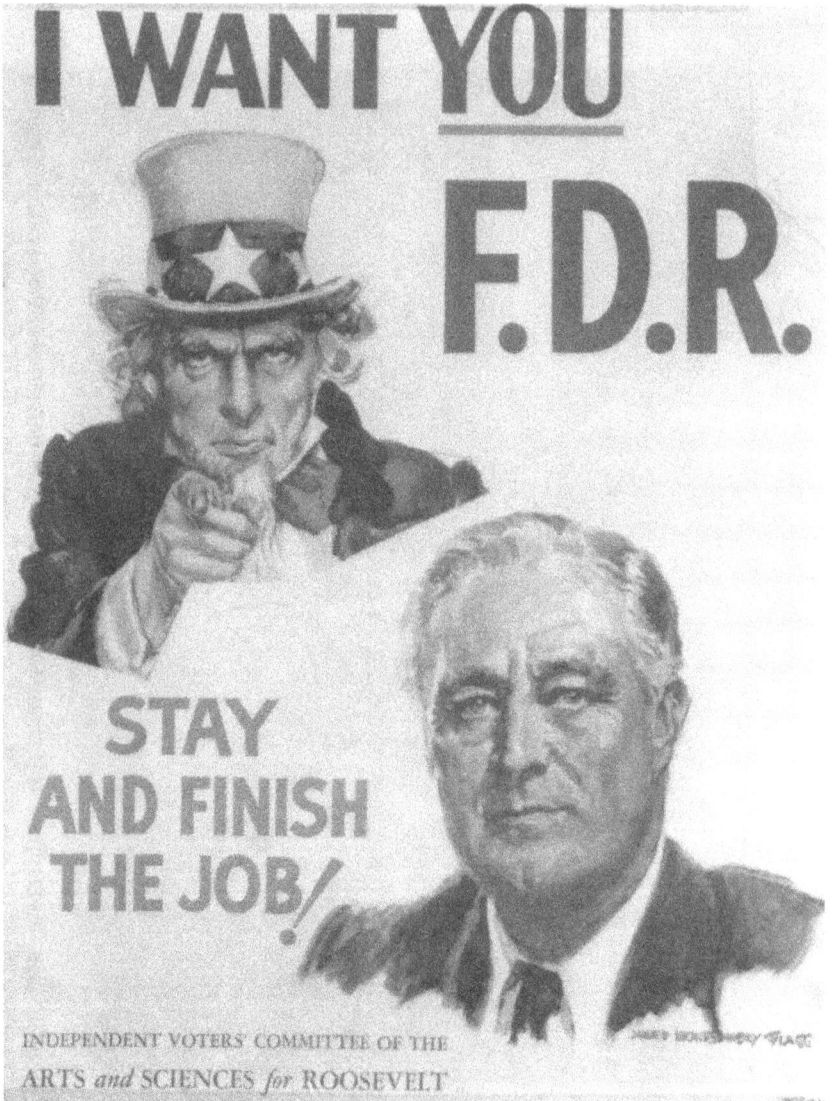

Fig. 16. The third term issue divided Americans as much as any event during Roosevelt's presidency. Credit: Franklin D. Roosevelt Library.

Fig. 17. At a picnic for journalists in 1933, Roosevelt prepares to slice the NRA watermelon. Credit: AP/Wide World Photos.

Fig. 18. A run on a bank in Millbury, Massachusetts, in 1930. Credit: UPI/Bettmann Archive.

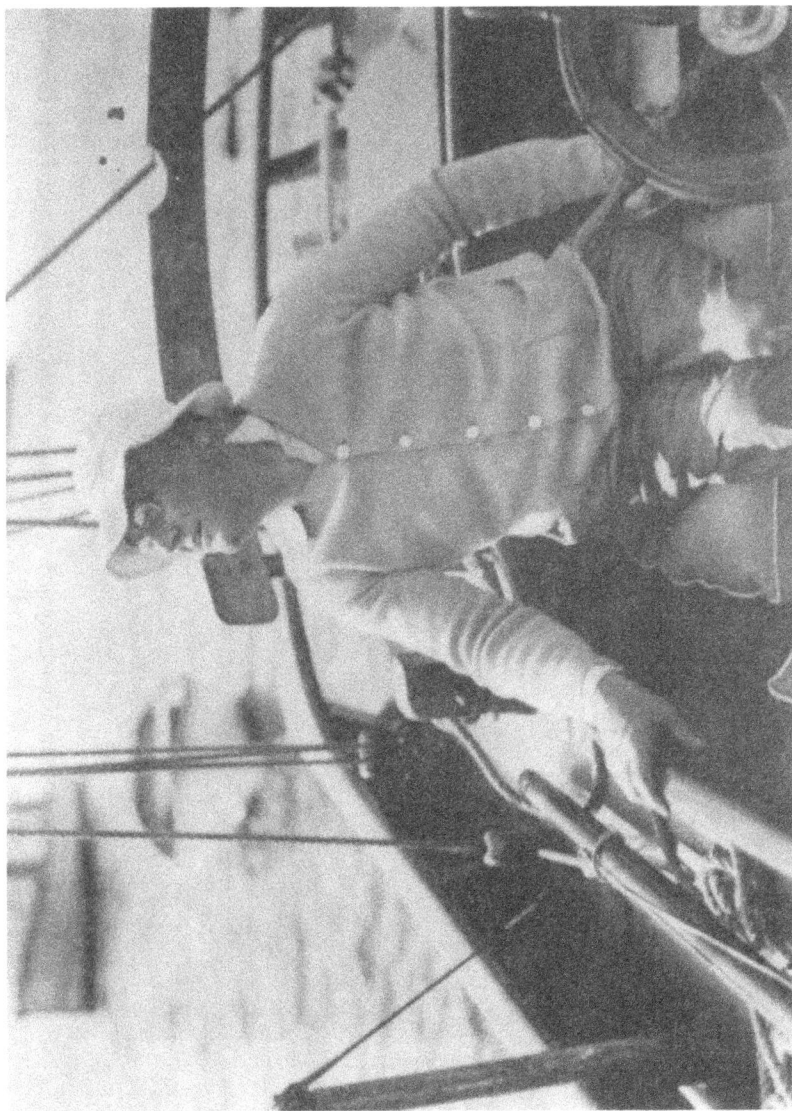

Fig. 19. Roosevelt relaxes on cruise in the summer of 1933. Credit: UPI/Bettmann Archive.

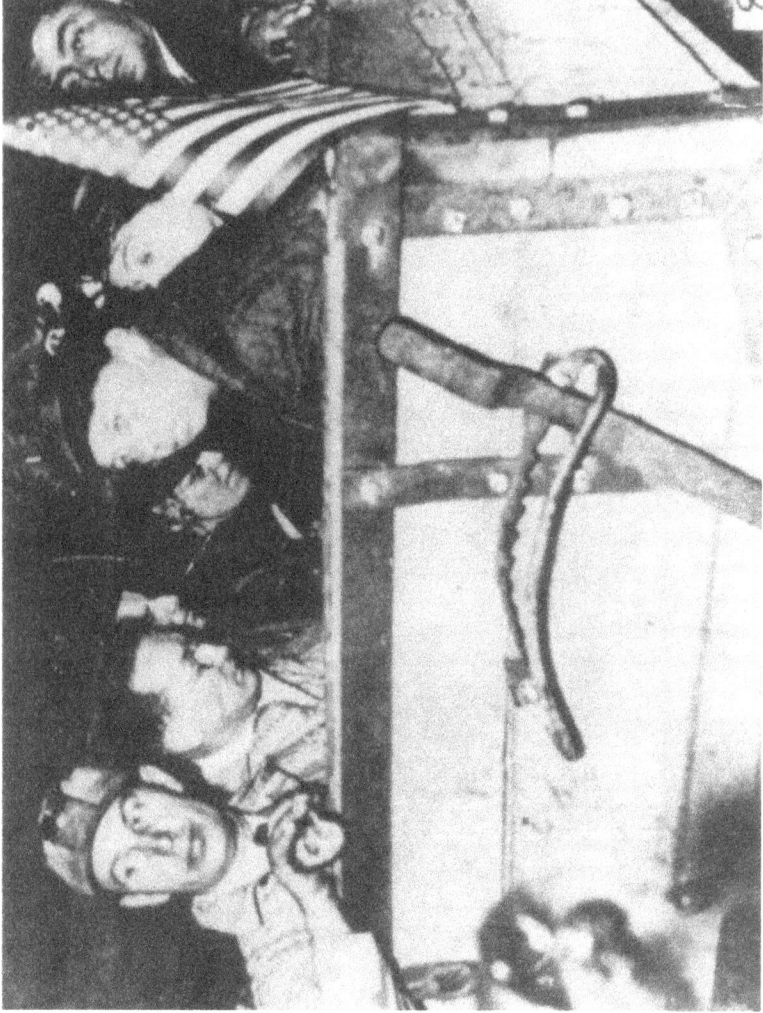

Fig. 20. Mrs. Roosevelt went almost anywhere, including a coal mine in Ohio in 1935. Credit: UPI/Bettmann Archive.

# 5

# The Focus

Without question, the center and the focal point of the 1930s and the New Deal was Franklin D. Roosevelt, the man. With possibly the exception of Abraham Lincoln, no other public figure has evoked so much emotion and been studied as much. Even today, some fifty years after his death, we are still grappling with who this man was and what he meant to American life.

Roosevelt was indeed an enigma. He was of patrician birth, a man who had few cares in life, and one who would not be expected to take a leading role in public affairs. He was from one of the old Dutch families from the Hudson Valley who was one of the most loved men in the South, possibly second only to Robert E. Lee. In his early life he was considered by many as a lightweight intellectually who tried to walk in the limelight of his cousin Theodore, but who was a pale reflection of this illustrious relative.

He was stricken with a childhood disease while a young adult and was promptly forgotten and ruled out as a future player in public life. Yet, with the aid and prompting of his indefatigable wife, Eleanor, he fought his way back to health. Although he never recovered the use of his legs, he became a robust man who caused others to forget about or ignore his handicap.

In his public life, no one engendered more extremes of emotion than Roosevelt. No one, it seems, had a neutral opinion of him. Everyone seemed either to love him or hate him; there seemed to be no middle ground. At least until his death, those who loved him far outnumbered his enemies.

Thus, any study of the 1930s has to take into account this man Roosevelt. Events swirled around him, and he stirred up much of the dust himself. At the beginning of his presidency—and even before—the most vocal were those who loved him, or at least had great hope and faith in what he could do for the country. His enemies were there, but they were fairly quiet at first. As the years passed and some of his programs became controversial, the Roosevelt haters became more visible and more vocal. The enemies will be the subject of chapter 8.

Here the Roosevelt supporters are the subject. Almost from the time he became governor of New York and the depression worsened under President Hoover, Democrats around the country began to look to Roosevelt as the Democratic candidate in 1932, and they were not shy about telling him of their trust and hopes. To be sure, there were other Democrats who wanted the nomination, including Alfred Smith, the former governor of New York and the Democratic candidate who lost to Hoover in 1928, and John Nance Garner, a long-time Texas politician and speaker of the House of Representatives. There were other potential candidates as well. In the pre-convention period, Roosevelt was, in some ways, a long shot, but he used many modern techniques and eventually received the nomination. Garner was chosen as the vice presidential candidate.

Roosevelt began breaking tradition right away, a practice he continued for the rest of his life. He flew to the convention and accepted the nomination in person, something that had not been done before. He said the crisis of the depression was so serious that playing coy and following custom would not do. He was straightforward and said the battle had to begin immediately.

Prior to and during the campaign the poets of the era poured out their praise for Roosevelt. Most of the time they were not very original in their sentiments, but, clearly, the great trust of Roosevelt is evident. They were captivated by his optimism and buoyancy, especially in contrast to Hoover, who became more dour as the economic news worsened week after week.

During the campaign a man from Phoenix, Arizona, alluded to Roosevelt's breaking of tradition and his qualities as a leader.

> It's a President they'er looking for,
> With intestinal strength to stand
> For things his own Country wants,
> One hundered Per Cent--- A- M A N.

> They want him,they'll get him,
> A General they can trust-
> His name is Franklin D. Roosevelt,
> They'll have him or bust.

> He entered an Airship,
> THE WAY HE WENT
> To tell the Convention-
> Delegations, their energy spent

"THIS CONVENTION IS FOR REPEAL".
Delegates APPLAUDED here and there
"I ACCEPT YOUR PLATFORM 100 PER CENT"
It spread like-ROARING MAGIC-everywhere.

Militant-they are-the people,
Ballot battling their enemy-gloom,
To kill existing conditions-
And sawt those Wall Street booms.[1]

A campaign song from a woman in Kentucky talked about Roosevelt's qualities of leadership.

Vote for Roosevelt he's the man,
    Save the country while you can,
The Roosevelt stock is pure as gold,
    He comes from ancestors fierce and bold.
. . . . . . . . . . . . . . . . . . . . . .
Surely our country is in a rut,
    Let's have a man that's got a gut,
And not afraid to say he's wet,
    The whole nation is waiting for such a bet.

A patriot who's bold and strong,
    For such an one, we've waited long,
We've dilly-dallied long enough,
    With hooch, that is such rotten stuff.[2]

A seventh-grade girl, also from Kentucky, talked about Roosevelt the person in the chorus of her campaign song which she set to the tune of "Yankee Doodle Dandy."

Roosevelt is our man,
Roosevelt is dandy.
He is the best, and very best,
And Roosevelt is handy.[3]

Another poet from Arizona may have summed up what a lot of people thought during the campaign.

I'm happy we have a leader like we have in Franklin D.,
I never was much at singing, I never could hit the key.

But you bet on your life I'm singing this song for Franklin D.
And you bet on your life I'm banking on Franklin D.'s regime.
Let's buckle right down to business—Let us work just like a team.
I never was much on working when nobody paid my time,
But you bet on your life I'm banking on Franklin D's regime.
And you bet on your life I'm ready to buckle in this time.

Oh Franklin D. is a powerful man, a little bit stern sometime,
But that's the kind of man we need to straighten out the times.
We never thought once of a Roosevelt till the kiddies began to
    cry—
But now we're banking on Franklin D., both wet and dry;
We never thought once of a team vote till we heard a Franklin
    Roosevelt theme.
But now united the country wide—we're all for Franklin D.[4]

When Roosevelt took office in March 1933, he took decisive action
in the executive area as had not been seen in America before. Between
the election in November 1932 and the inauguration in March 1933 was
a long period of waiting. Roosevelt refused to cooperate with President
Hoover on the few occasions he offered the opportunity, something most
presidents-elect had always done. He was not about to be linked in the
public mind with any Hoover policy or initiative. With the seriousness of
the economic crisis, the incoming administration was champing at the bit
to get into power and begin to do things. The public was just as ready for
action.

During the long interim, many of the poets found their anticipation
growing and were expecting dramatic action. Roosevelt did not
disappoint them. A whirlwind of activity and a blizzard of legislation
were forthcoming.

When the action began, the poets who liked Roosevelt were ecstatic.
A man from New Jersey wrote a poem he entitled "The Great Eman-
cipator" in which he expressed these opinions.

Roosevelt is here
So banish all fear!
With might and main
He'll battle and gain--
He'll strive and strain
To reach the main!
With a mighty attack,
He'll bring us back!

Where we were once before
On Solid Shore!

So help Him fight--
To reach the height!
And uphold the hands
That are untying the strands!
Of want and dispair--
Of misery and care--
And aid him in his battle grand--
To free this great and glorious land!
For Roosevelt is here
Do not fear.[5]

On inauguration day, a Georgian living in Pasadena, California, carefully wrote by hand on a postcard a poem entitled "Our New President." On the bottom of the card he wrote, in reference to Mrs. Roosevelt, "We love her out here and you know how we all but worship you in Georgia."[6] The poem reflected the hope that some people had in Roosevelt.

Tears rose in hardened eyes--from mine they flowed--
When Franklin Roosevelt's inaugural vow
Broadcast its purpose, with the help of God,
To lift our Country from Depression's slough.
There was a note of action in his voice
That put a prick in Unemployment's ear,
And made our Nation's flagging soul rejoice
With a new hope that a new deal was near.
    The creaking doors of trade throughout the earth
Must needs be oiled. Full-front he shall be turning
His zeal that way, when on each darkened hearth
Home action shall have set our home fires burning.
Here spake a President! Here spake a man!--
American and cosmopolitan.[7]

Later in 1933, a Californian expressed the love she had for Roosevelt and what she believed others felt about him.

God bless you, Mr. President!
We're with you to a man.
Where others said, "Impossible,"

You smiled and said, "WE CAN!"
You pointed out the path ahead
For us to follow on;
You found us in the darkest night
And brought us to the dawn.

We thank you, Mr. President.
We've found a friend in you.
You're for us and you're one of us;
You have no chosen few.
For your heart is with the people,
It knows no class nor clan.
At last we've found our leader--
A true American.

We love you, Mr. President;
We love you with our hearts.
You've done your best to help us
And now we'll do our parts.
And all of us together
With our shoulders to the wheel,
Will push and work and back you up
With patriotic zeal.

God bless you, Mr. President,
And all you aim to do.
America is with her leader.
On! We're following you![8]

The optimism was so great during Roosevelt's first hundred days that a woman believed, incorrectly, that Roosevelt had ended the depression in America.

Three cheers for Roosevelt
    The pride of our nation
Who is bringing prosperity
    To hungry men and relation
Their hearts were filled with sadness
    But, now they have changed to gladness
We are standing on the quay
    Everybody's happy
On Roosevelt day

We have buried old depression
  In the bottom of the Sea
    Those gloomy days
Soon will be forgotten
    When the sunlight shines
      For you and me.[9]

    Only a few days after the inauguration a poet wrote some verses for a hosiery mill in Indianapolis, Indiana, that praised the new administration to the tune of the popular song, "Frankie and Johnnie."

    Frankie and Johnnie are leaders,
    Chosen to run this great land!
    Now they're down at the capitol
    Let's give 'em a great big hand!
Chorus: Because they're our men--they won't do us wrong!

    Frankie went down to the White House,
    Wearin' a big silk hat;
    He took it off there, and rolled up his sleeves
    And stepped right up to bat!
Chorus: He is our man--and he'll do us right!

    Now take ol' John Nance Garner,
    His friends call him "Cactus Jack";
    He's a man we can always count on
    'Cause a Texan never turns his back!
Chorus: He is a man--and he'll do us right!

    Frankie wrote down to Congress,
    A-tellin' 'em where to head in;
    An' what he said made 'em act mighty quick
    It must 'a been good medicine!
Chorus: They knew their man--they dassn't do him wrong!

    Johnnie went down to the Senate,
    To take full charge of those boys;
    He rapped his gavel once or twice
    And they stopped their crazy noise!
Chorus: They saw their boss--they didn't fool him long!

So we got ol' Frankie and Johnnie,
To run our Ship of State;
They've taken holt in a way we like
An' we're goin' to celebrate!
Chorus: They are our men--they won't do us wrong![10]

When Congress passed the National Industrial Recovery Act (NIRA) in 1933, a great surge of hope spread throughout the country. In a poem praising the NIRA, an author from Detroit, Michigan, praised Roosevelt.

We've chosen a captain, fearless and bold
With oceans of courage stored in the hold
He's now at the helm, going full speed
Guiding the ship over teacherous seas.

The crew are all stalwart battle scarred men.
They know the ropes from the prow to the stern
Storms are but trifles to this gallant crew
Their live's have been given to see this thing through

The passenger list, it makes us feel proud
Celebrities great and others a crowd
They're pulling together all with a vim
Now board the ship Nira and help us to win.[11]

A short time later a poet from New Jersey could not praise Roosevelt enough.

Genius has placed its mark upon his brow;
And there is gentle courage in his smile;
To guage his worth, one need but look upon
His eyes, wherein's the wisdom of the Nile![12]

A poignant expression of what people were thinking about Roosevelt's success was a song written in 1933 by a poet from Terre Haute, Indiana.

I heard a sweet voice as I passed on my way
'Twas the voice of a sweet little girl.
Who was nursing her doggie and prattling so gay
Her words put my head in a whirl
"Now doggie dear, doggie you listen to me,

I'll tell you a story that's true
Be quiet--don't lick me--and soon you will see,
It's the goodest news I'm telling you.

Oh, Daddy has gone back to work
Dear Daddy has gone back to work
Did you get what I said
In your little dumb head,
I say Daddy has gone back to work."

We'll have lots of good things to eat doggie dear,
And we'll never be hungry and blue
I'm so glad and so happy--quit licking my ear--
And please hold your tongue till I'm thru
We'll have lots of goodies, pie, jelly and cake
Sweet pudding and candy and cones
And maybe fried chicken, then if you're real good,
You may get some nice fried chicken bones.[13]

Roosevelt often was compared to other people, especially American heroes from another age. Lincoln was viewed by many as the person who saved the United States from dissolution during the Civil War. It was a small step to comparing Roosevelt to Lincoln because to many of the poets Roosevelt was saving the United States from a similar crisis. In 1934 a poet from Brooklyn wrote a poem he called "We Have Another Lincoln Down in Washington."

There is a little town called Hyde Park in New York State,
Franklin Roosevelt came from there a noble candidate,
He was elected president in the thickest of the fray,
Just like Abraham Lincoln was when he saved the day,
Frank's new deal has made a change,
It banished all our woes,
He's another Lincoln everybody knows.

We have another Lincoln down in Washington,
His name is Franklin Roosevelt and he is loved by everyone,
We will keep him in the White House, for the good work he has done,
We need Franklin Roosevelt down in Washington.

Our land was in an awful mess ever since the war,
The people all felt sore when depression hit their door,
We elected Roosevelt to straighten all things out,
Now everybody's happy and with praise for him they shout.[14]

A Texan, in a birthday poem to Roosevelt, compared him to Lincoln, but he threw in Woodrow Wilson as well.

Born of Faith and Washington,
Young Columbia arose,
Lincoln saved her as a son;
Died amid her civil throes.

Wilson, too, was martyred here;
Counted wise beyond his age.
Roosevelt comes without a fear,
Triumps over Midas' gauge.

Unto Us a child is born;
Franklin Roosevelt shall he be.
Fate seems jealous of that morn;
Smites him, body, arm and knee.

Vaiantly he meets that foe,
Scorning dread paralysis;
Simulating, as we know,
God's creative genesis.

Rising as a president,
Roosevelt leads where others shrink;
Halts Depression's downward bent,
Saves a nation on the brink.[15]

A man from Chicago added several American heroes including Washington and Tom Paine in a long poem. Four verses bring in other American leaders from the past.

If Jefferson were here today,
He'd be the frist to back you,
And score the lies of royalists,
Now trying to attack you.

Were Andrew Jackson with us now,
That dauntless doughty fighter,
Would now be fighting at your side,
To make your burden lighter.

Were peerless Patrick Henery here,
To hear their legal edicts,
He'd raise his matchless voice in scorn,
To answer all your critics.

Those are the heros of the past,
Who fought the fight before you
They are gone, and yet we know
Their spirit hovers o'r you.[16]

Probably the person most poets compared Roosevelt to was Moses, who led the Israelites out of slavery in Egypt into the promised land. He had to contend with non-believers and contention within his own ranks. Roosevelt was leading the American people out of the slavery of the depression, but he had to contend with similar conflicts from within the public.

A man from Ohio recounted the problems the country was facing, but then he concluded on an uplifting note.

But like Moses in the good story so old,
A champion has risen,who with action bold
Will lead us out of our unscrupulous ways,
Back to the thought that unselfishness pays.[17]

A man from Illinois did much the same thing. He sketched the problems and then compared Roosevelt to Moses. But he also projected into the future.

And then arose a man of might
A modern Moses bold,
To release the people from their plight
A conscious man with heart of gold.

Gifted with wisdom and power of speech
Yet not content with words alone,
He put in action what he did preach,
He fed the hungry and saved the home.

Before one day had fairly set
He put in motion his campaign,
And never in this nation yet
Has a President earned such fame.

. . . . . . . . . . . . . . . . . .

Men of brains he mobilized,
All experts in their line,
The brain trust, they were stigmatized
By pigmies in combine.

With wisdom keen and vision rare
He marshalled all his force
Those who faltered were sent to the rear
And he never altered his course.

There yet remains so much to do
But the ship is under weigh,
And with his trusty able crew
The sailing's clear today.

And in the years to come we'll see
His noble record on history's pages,
Calamity he turned to victory,
Roosevelt lives through the ages.[18]

A woman from Laredo, Texas, got carried away with rhymes and the Moses analogy.

Oh Roosevelt, art thou a Moses,
To lead this poor nation
Whose sad purse deflation
Has caused much vexation,
And hot altercation,
Not to mention starvation?
Oh Roosevelt, art though this Moses?

I say, art thou the Moses
On whose reputation
We're promised salvation,
And tax regulation?
Is job consideration

Thine own specialization?
Thou art indeed this Moses!

Hail Democrat Moses!
Accept our ovation;
Excuse it's duration,
And our agitation,
And attempted versification.
Your administration
I hail, Democrat Moses![19]

In a long poem from Long Beach, California, a poet included both Moses and Jesus Christ in his praise of Roosevelt.

The Big Boys were on their knees,
    waiting for the end
Asking God to help them,
    and save them from their fate
Send a man to lead us,
    before it is too late.
After their prayers were answered,
    like Biblical times of old
When Moses led the Israelites,
    to safety, and to the fold
They even had a Judas,
    and so it came about
That Jesus the Son of God,
    they could no longer doubt
Was the Leader of the Masses,
    he stood for what was right
He was the only perfect man,
    and had a halo of light
Around his head and shoulders,
    it plainly could be seen
But he also had enemies,
    whose hatred had turned green
And so it is with Roosevelt,
    after all that he has done
They try to take the credit,
    after the battle has been won[20]

Some of the poets went further and compared Roosevelt to Jesus and God or, short of that, said that Roosevelt was chosen by God or that some other divine authority selected Roosevelt for his task. An example came from a lengthy poem by a woman from North Carolina.

> Our Heavenly God has blessed us, and Roosevelt has dressed us,
> Blessed be our God and our King.
> When you're feeling lonely, don't forget to sing,
> Blessed be our God and our King.
> Jesus Christ has led us, and Roosevelt has fed us,
> Blessed be our God and our King.
> When you're feeling lonely, don't forget to sing,
> Blessed be our God and our King.[21]

This poem goes on for several verses in the same vein.
    Another example came from a woman from Ohio.

> so in the silent night when every
> one was at rest and Slumbered.
> Jesus dispatched his people a leader
> who would help them out of distress.
> the rich as well as the poor
> in a world of depression so long we
> have trod our sins will be moved when
> we stand up for Jesus as in
> Long long years ago.
>
> We all shall remember the years of
> thirty one two and three . . . . for the world
> was depressed more than we ever
> did see . . . until Mr. Roosevelt
> through Jesus brought us liberty so
> dear people if we trust in Jesus
> the NRA will land us saftely on shore.[22]

Another woman from Ohio put it this way.

> We know you must be a man, put there by god
> for this good work. no other man have tried.
> When you have something in mind to do.
> You never stoped, until you saw it through.
> Mr Roosevelt Mr Roosevelt we surly are proud of you.[23]

A veterans' organization from New Jersey published a poem in preparation for the presidential convention of 1936, in which Roosevelt was seeking a second term. The role of God in Roosevelt's career and in the life of the United States is clear in some of the lines of the poem, which is quoted in full here.

> Tis truly said of God indeed,
> He finds the man to suit the need.
>
> He saw our plight in 'Thirty-two,
> When things looked black for me and you,
> And so He sent a man to reign,
> Tried in His crucible of pain,
> A smiling man, one unafraid
> To face the crisis undismayed;
> A man who spoke in homely terms
> And thought of us as men not worms,
> A man who told the haughty few
> Just what they could and could not do.
> A man who did not know it all,
> But said instead "We'll try our best
> And then to God leave all the rest."
>
> His best was good, he kept his vow.
> We trust him more than ever now.[24]

A man from Washington, D.C., sent a poem entitled "The Almighty Lord's Selection," in which he talked about the role that God played in Roosevelt's actions.

> HE began to investigate the great and the small
> And selected from the Human-beings the best of all
> He selected FRANKLIN D. ROOSEVELT as his helper
> To provide all Human-beings with food and shelter
>
> HE was sure that ROOSEVELT would give him action
> To lead his people in the right direction
> He was sure that ROOSEVELT would work without a rest
> For his people and his Country's best
>
> HE was sure that ROOSEVELT would obey the LORD'S instruction
> To save the UNITED STATES from a sure destruction

He gave him orders to use his wondrous skill
And fulfill the ALMIGHTY LORD'S wish and will[25]

A man from Los Angeles mentioned how close Roosevelt was to God.

His thoughtful eyes reflect Olympian heights,-
But with his feet firm planted on earth's sod;
That like Sir Galahad, with soul so pure,
Men say: "Our champion walks with God!"[26]

A poet from Florida believed Roosevelt's place in history was determined by God.

When Washington's stones lie cold in dust,
When our last Battleship is a pile of rust,
When the Flag itself has ceased to wave,
When America is just one Grave:
    If there is a God there still shall stand,
    One name undying o'er the land,
And in God's heart a thrill be felt,
For FRANKLIN DELANO ROOSEVELT!.[27]

Others made religious references while advising and praising Roosevelt in other ways. In 1935 a woman from Florida talked about Roosevelt feeding the lambs.

Have you forgotten your Father in Heaven?
Do you read the book that He has given?
Read it and say your prayers;
Good blessings will come instead of tares.

Have you closed your heart and purse the same?
Open each I pray in the Saviour's name,
Help your neighbor, give him a hand;
"Feed my sheep," was the Lord's command.

Roosevelt is our leader, don't let him fall;
He's trying to help you, He's trying to help all.
"Feed my lambs," was the Lord's command;
Do your part, Brother; help him to stand.

Come on everybody, now is the time;
Help Roosevelt save our country, don't pull back and whine:
There is joy for everybody if you'll only lend a hand,
He has the wisdom our Father gave him;
Won't you help him feed the lambs?[28]

Some of the other poets advised Roosevelt to be brave and to stay the course, despite the critics that were more vocal by 1935.

To our Captain, brave and fearless, who is holding fast the helm,
    Keep your courage and your eye upon the Star!
It will lead us to the "Haven of Prosperity" once more,
    We have faith in you and know you as you are!
God's eternal mills grind slowly but they grind exceeding small--
    Time is ever reaching upward to the height--
What today is trampled on and beaten in the dust,
    Tomorrow shall,triumphant, see the light![29]

Among people who liked Roosevelt, the admiration was almost unlimited. This is that element of Roosevelt's personality that historians have grappled with for years. All presidents have their supporters, but the admiration usually is limited to support for positions and programs. The desperation of the depression may have caused people to look for someone they could believe understood the problems of everyone. Roosevelt certainly filled that bill.

A man from San Antonio, Texas, clearly expressed this opinion.

We hail you, Franklin Roosevelt,
    You are a prince and king!
Despite all satan's forces
    You'll do the essential thing.
You can be depended on;
    Your courage never fails,
With your hand upon the helm
    We'll dare all seas to sail.

We need a leader of your type -
    A man of truest blue,
A man in whom trust does abide,
    Confidence and honor, too.
Our faith so many had abused,

> Our ranks were in dispair,
> But we feel God's hand is o'er the land
>   Since you are in the chair.
>
> Our needs you fully comprehend,
>   No storm escapes your eye;
> We know you'll lead us to the end -
>   Under you we'll do or die.
> You took control and now you hold
>   Our fate within your hand,
> We look to you and trust you, too,
>   The ship of state to land.[30]

The common people of America thought Roosevelt understood them and that they had a personal connection to him. An employee of the Civil Works Administration (CWA) in Virginia believed Roosevelt was his friend.

> We are digging in the C. W. A.
> To get money our debts to pay.
> Oh what a pain.
> Our debtors have begun to holler,
> Come thou almighty dollar,
> We need the change.
>
> But I began to think I guess,
> That I am not by myself;
> I try to sing.
> Go thou almighty dollar.
> You have been well spent;
> I could have used you in Hoover's time,
> To paid on my rent.
>
> When I cross the Silent River
> I hope I can sing;
> And all my debts on earth are paid,
> Before I meet my King.
> Then I will pray to the Lord of Host,
> For He knows my end,
> To send praises to Roosevelt, most,
> FOR HE IS MY FRIEND.[31]

Some of the poets looked upon Roosevelt as a relative who cared about humanity and brought freedom to the people.

> He came to us as a brother
>    who asked to be given the might
>    to be our leader and thinker
>    to restore our national rights.
> He established a code for the takers
>    to return their illogical gains
>    thus increasing the wage of the makers
>    who thereby would share in their aims....
>
> We have a leader and thinker
>    we follow the lead of his aims
>    we follow the lead of his visions
>    that opens the rights for our claims.
> Tremble Oh Shirkers and Takers!
>    Your gains will be crushed by your greed.
> The Star Spangled Banner is waving
>    where millions of men have been freed....[32]

Many of the poets simply talked about Roosevelt's human qualities and his concern for people of all kinds. A man from New York City said it this way:

> The day you were inaugerated I never shall forget,
> To the humble heart of millions it meant true happeness.
> Who for years have been down trodden with hard work and little
>    pay,
> Knew you'd stop the explotation through the famous N.R.A.
>
> Oh blast you false philosophers who lust for greed and gain,
> You robbed this entire country great riches to obtain.
> But by an act of Providence where justice still remains,
> The man now in the White House treats the rich and poor the
>    same.[33]

A woman from Portland, Oregon, wrote a poem, which was published in a local newspaper. She was adamant in her feeling.

> They scoff and they laugh at the things he has done;
> They've sneered at each new thing that he has begun;

But the fact still remains that my family now
Has clothing, and shelter, and food, and somehow
I feel that I'd like to just tell him that we,
As a family, think that his motives we see.

It seems to us now, as we look at years past,
That we've got as a leader a neighbor at last.
We feel that our troubles he makes his, in part--
A man who is human--a man with a heart!
We think if we met him he'd clasp both our hands
And tell us our struggles he well understands.

So we'd just like to thank him for what he has done,
For this family a happier life has begun;
We have a new hope as we look down the years
To the dawn of a day of less sorrow and tears,
And we feel in our hearts he'll still do all he can
To brighten the path of the Forgotten Man.[34]

A woman from Indiana talked about the president's feelings about people.

There's a difference in the People
Since depression stalked the land
They are doing their own thinking
And they'er closer clasping hand.
Like the rolling of the sea
When the tide is coming in
They are moving closer, closer
To the cause they want to win
Yes the U.S.A. is Happier
Joy and Hope are Everywhere
Since our Country has a President
With the Capacity to Care.

In this country folks existed
Some conditions were like hell
No security were they offered
Though they served the rich men well
Till the riches all were gathered
In the hands of very few.
Parents jobless, children hungry.

Cursed cause Nothing they could do.
Now they work and they are happy
Joy and Hope are Everywhere.
Since our Country has a President
With the Capacity to Care[35]

Some of the poets saw this human touch in his concern and assistance
for the weak in society. Because of his own illness and his regular visits
to Warm Springs, Georgia, some people had a special feeling for him. In
1935 one of the poets printed a poem extolling Roosevelt's virtues,
obviously in preparation for the reelection campaign of 1936.

You never forgot the weak nor the poor
Bounteous blessings are laid at your door.
Through your vision and foresight, world renowned,
Relief for the hungry and homeless, you've found.

Your beneficence, like angel's wings,
Enfolds the helpless at "Warm Springs".
Noble-hearted and full of love--
To them you are divine, sent from above.[36]

A man from San Jose, California, was especially appreciative of
Roosevelt's work with crippled children.

My heart aches for Children that suffer
And struggle for health in vain
But there is one who is kind and helpful
With no thought of earthly gain

He is doing great things for these Children
His all he would gladly give
Toward the science and tender care
That these may have a chance to live

He carries a load that is greater
Than any of whom I know
With a smile and a hand that is willing
To help those that disease has lain low

No reward will seem quite sufficient
For the kind deeds he has done

So we give three cheers for Our President
A man that is second to none[37]

As the reelection campaign of 1936 approached, the poets waxed
eloquently about Roosevelt's achievements. They talked about what he
had done and derided his critics. A woman from Missouri expressed her
sentiments to the popular tune "Old Black Joe."

Gone are the days when depression laid us low,
Gone are the fears of the people, this we know;
Gone from the dole to better times, by far;
We hear again our nation's call for F.D.R.

We need him, we need him,
For his great heart beats for all,
We hear again the people call for F.D.R.

We need him, we need him,
For his great humanity,
We hear again the people call for F.D.R.[38]

A woman from Ohio exhorted Democrats to do their duty.

Oh we have a Democrat President
Why can't we keep that Democrat President
For there's not another man
Who can equal in this land
With our own Roosevelt and his Plans.

Oh he has helped us all far and near
To our country and to us he's a dear
He will help us more I know
If we our appreciation show
And elect him president again this year.

I know you are good Democrats too
So why should all of us be in a stew
When at the polls you are
Just make Roosevelt your star.
And we'll show them what the Democrats can do.[39]

To a high school student from Colorado, the reason the voters should support Roosevelt was obvious.

> Our President is behind us and is holding us up.
> And if it wasn't for him we would surely blow up.
> So boost up boys, let's try to grow hay
> And support our President on election day.[40]

When speculation about who the candidates might be in 1936 was heating up, a poet from Rhode Island considered several possibilities and rejected them all.

> IT WONT BE NO CHARLIE COUGHLIN, OH--
> WITH, HIS SOCIAL ARMY--AND--FLEET--
> FOR HE TALKS A STRANGE STORY--LANGUAGE--
> THAT--PEOPLE JUST CANT--MAKE OUT--
>
> AND, IT WONT BE SIR TOWNSEND, OH, NEION
> WITH ODLES AND ODLES OF DOUGH--
> WHERE IN THE WORLD WOULD THE MONEY COME FROM--
> FOR, THE FREE BURSTING- BURST PURSE OH, GEE--
>
> AND IT WONT BE, AL, SMITH- OF THE SIDEWALK
> HE MAY JUST AS WELL SAY QUIT--
> FOR, TWO OR THREE YEARS HE HAS TRIED IT--
> BUT, AL, HAS ALWAYS, BEEN LICKED--
>
> IT, WONT BE MR, HOOVER WE,LL TAKE CARE OF THAT--
> FOR HIS CHANCES HAVE PASSED HIM BYE--
> HIS GREEN GRASS, PREDICTIONS ALL HIS GLOOMINESS--
> JUST MEANS, THIS HES LAID ON THE SHELF--
>
> AND, IT WONT BE MR, TALMADGE- OH ME--OH MY--
> I,VE HEARD HIM TALK ON THE MIKE--
> THE THINGS THAT HE SAID SOUNDED SILLY--
> AND, T,IS WISDOM WE NEED IN THE NATION TO, DAY--
>
> AND, THE G,O,P, HAVE PICKED A PEACH--
> WHO, LOOKS LIKE FRANKLIN D,--
> THE GENTLEMAN MAY BE ALL RIGHT--
> BUT , J, HENRY SMYTHE IS NOT FRANKLIN D,
> SO,

;SO, WE WILL NOT FALL FOR NICE FACES--
.TIS THE HEART OF MAN WE CANT SEE--
FOR, IN FOUR YEARS, THERE,S BEEN PEACE FOLKS--
AND, IN THE YEARS TO COME , WISH THIS TO BE--[41]

As the campaign heated up, a woman from Independence, Missouri, wrote a poem supporting Roosevelt. She described herself as "a widow, who has no other help, or means to live only by working for the WPA at the sewing room. So she gives him all the praise."[42]

> We will sing the wonderous words of praise,
> For the one who has served us well;
> For the one who will save our nation
> From the depths we cannot tell.
>
> If we all will stick together,
> What a day of rejoicing that will be;
> When we re-elect Roosevelt-
> We will sing and shout the victory.
>
> He is the one whose hand has fed us;
> Through his works and ways of trust;
> Trhough his toils of hope and vigor,
> We must help to do him just.
>
> With his help we have clothed our children,
> Saved our homes through the endless days;
> Now we must not forget our duties
> Through our work of hope and praise.
>
> Now, we all must do our duty
> For the one who has helped us all;
> Then we will not forget his kindness;
> When he needs our help this coming fall.[43]

A man from Ohio encouraged the voters not to forget what Roosevelt had done when they went to the polls.

> Now, how you gonna vote?
> How you gonna vote?
> How you gonna vote? I say,
> Don't be a big monkey
> On election day.

Now let us see,
Old Franklin D.,
Back in '33
He waded in up to his chin,
To rescue you and me.

He rescued you,
He rescued me,
He put us on our feet,
Don't - go - high-hat now,
When you meet him on the street.[44]

Roosevelt won the election of 1936 with the largest popular and electoral majority ever. The Republican candidate, Alfred Landon, carried only Maine and Vermont. The people clearly were still with Roosevelt.

By the time Roosevelt decided to break tradition and run for a third term in 1940, some of the ardor for him had cooled. Many people were outraged that he would be arrogant enough to try to do what no other president had done. He lost support even among many hard-core Democrats. Even so, he won again quite easily.

The poets were not as active in the 1940 campaign as they had been earlier, but a few still sang his praises. Even before the dust had settled after the victory in 1936 a woman from Chicago was advocating a third term.

You have stood for rebuke
Time and again,
With malice towards none
But a determined cain
Shows them how easy it is to win.
A third term, Roosevelt.
. . . . . . . . . . . . . . . . .
Wisdom like yours
Made history anew
C O N S T E R A T I O N speaks only too true
Franklin Delano Roosevelt
A third term with the Red White and Blue.
And the band will keep playing
YANKEE DOO DLE DOO.[45]

By the fall of 1939 another poem appeared supporting the third term.

The Jefferson of our day,
Standard-bearer 'f U.S.A.
People's Champ of near and far
Three Cheers, Three Terms for F.D.R.

Battling hatred, greed and bane,
With reaction put to shame.
A noble Record at people's bar,
Three Cheers, Three Terms for F.D.R.

A Happy Home is Roosevelt's goal,
With Prosperity for all, so.....
Let's hitch the wagon to our guiding star,
and LET US KEEP OUR F.D.R.

So with our shoulder to the wheel,
We shall fight for his New Deal.
Keep the Whitehouse door ajar:
Three Cheers, Three Terms For F.D.R.[46]

The enthusiasm for Roosevelt of a man from Pennsylvania seemed unbounded.

President Roosevelt.
We felt you on the line.
We could not reach you in time,
To save us from the bread line.
Now we have you on the line.
We should keep you all the time.
At least until your 99.
So keep this in mind President Roosevelt.[47]

From the beginning Roosevelt had his critics, to be sure, and they grew more vocal and intense as time passed and opposition grew to his various New Deal programs. But throughout his life, and after his death, the praise continued. No president was ever more loved, and possibly more hated, than Roosevelt. The adoration is still a mystery and a thing of wonder for those who study Roosevelt and the New Deal.

# 6

# The New Deal

When Franklin Roosevelt became president in 1933, hopes were high in America. Roosevelt's upbeat campaign and optimistic inauguration address set a tone that had not been seen for some time. Roosevelt promised action, and he was not slow in delivering on the pledge.

Roosevelt had been praised by America's amateur poets while he was a candidate because they thought he could do something about the depression. The praise in verse continued throughout his presidency as one program after another was begun. The poets did not respond to all the programs and they were not always favorable to them. Some of the lesser-known or more technical programs—such as the Securities and Exchange Commission (SEC)—did not generate much poetry. Neither did the programs such as the Federal Writers Project that may have been viewed by the average poets as something that did not affect them.

The major New Deal programs did generate interest, especially those that were easy to understand and the ones that touched people directly. Often the poems inserted references to various agencies in a longer poem that was aimed primarily to praise Roosevelt. These were used primarily as examples of the many great things Roosevelt had done for the country. The poems dealing with New Deal agencies were numerous particularly during the Hundred Days and immediately thereafter as legislation poured out of Congress in a torrent never seen before. As some of the programs and agencies aged, they lost some of their luster, but even so, many poets never wavered in their support.

One of the programs that offered hope and promise and was promoted on a major scale by the White House was the National Recovery Administration (NRA). Created by the National Industrial Recovery Act (NIRA) on June 16, 1933, the last day of the Hundred Days session of Congress, the law was designed to restore business prosperity. Based on the idea of industrial self-regulation, businesses, under government supervision, developed codes of fair competition. In effect, the law suspended the antitrust laws and allowed for cooperation that had not been seen for years. Eventually some 500 fields of enterprise employing some 22 million people were affected. The NRA was headed by General Hugh S. Johnson.

Not only was business benefited by the NRA. Section 7a of the NIRA guaranteed the workers the right to organize and bargain collectively with their employers. Now for the first time organized labor was recognized in law. The workers now saw themselves as being supported by the government instead of being at the mercy of both employers and government.

Almost immediately the poets jumped to support the NRA. Since many of the poets were unsophisticated people with little knowledge of national events, they might be dismissed as people merely jumping on the bandwagon to support the New Deal. That would be a premature evaluation. The tone and content of many of the poems show the great hope many people had for the NRA and the fact that many believed they were helped by the agency.

Only four days after passage of the NIRA, a poem was mailed to Roosevelt praising the NRA and its symbol, the Blue Eagle. Clearly, this early this poet from New Jersey had no idea what the NRA might do. Instead she was appealing for support for the help it might bring. Two verses of the poem show the great hope she held.

> Hail to the Blue Eagle
>> Soaring so high
> Out of his nest
>> From the White House he flies.
>
> . . . . . . . . . . . . . . . . . .
> With outstretched wings
>> The Blue Eagle stands
> Waiting and listening
>> For Gen Johnson's command
> To return back home
>> In peace and content
> And tell President Roosevelt
>> The U.S. is with him
> One Hundred Per Cent.[1]

By late summer and early fall of 1933, as the outlines of the NRA began to emerge, more poets added their voices to the praise. In addition to the Blue Eagle as its symbol the NRA had a motto as well: "We Do Our Part." This motto, or variations of it, often was found in the poems. For example, in August 1933 a thirteen-year-old boy from Virginia said that America had to "pull together" and stand behind the NRA.

The N.R.A. The N.R.A.
United now we stand,
And we pledge our might,
In the cause of right,
For the blessing of our Native land,
So when you see these letters three
Remember what they say,
We will pull together always,
That's the motto of the N.-R.-A.[2]

A man who was clearly wealthy enough to have residences in Tampa, Florida, and Cambridge, Massachusetts, sent Roosevelt a poem to be sung as a song to the tune of "Mandalay." This poem reflected the emerging NRA and its promise. It also incorporated its motto.

We see them everywhere we go
Throughout the land today,
They bear a mighty message
Those letters N-R-A-
They instill in every patriot mind
A purpose and intent
To wage a worthy battle,
And support the president.

There' a code for every business,
For factory, farm and store.
It puts the issue up to all,
To do our part and more.
And each and every one must feel
The obligation strong
To purchase goods produced at home:
In this we can't go wrong.[3]

A consistent theme in the poems was to encourage people to support the NRA. An example was a poem from a man in Louisville, Kentucky.

If all would assist with a plan worth while,
then later we will wear a great big smile,
that plan, we call it the N.R.A.,
is mighty fine for the U.S.A.
If all in business will do their share,

> the workers can eat and have clothes to wear,
> then we can credit the emblem,N.R.A.,
> with being the savior of the U.S.A.
> This plan if aided by one and all,
> will place depression beyond recall,
> and later when we think of the N.R.A.,
> we'll say, what a blessing for the U.S.A.
> So why shirk a cause we all know is right,
> let us all start now and aid in the fight,
> knock old depression out with the N.R.A.,
> and make life worth living in the U.S.A.[4]

A man from Lockport, Illinois, incorporated the Blue Eagle and the motto in his poem promoting support for the NRA.

> It took the BLUE EAGLE to drive the blues away,
>     The NEW DEAL means good times will come to stay --
> So let's get going, and "DO OUR PART":
>     Back this program with all your heart.
> JOBS FOR THE NATION -- that's our goal --
>     More and more names on the old Pay Roll;
> Let's Go, America! We'll win the day-
>     IT TOOK THE BLUE EAGLE TO DRIVE THE BLUES AWAY.[5]

Some of these poets early in the life of the NRA seemed to feel the need to reassure Roosevelt that the people were with him and the NRA.

> President Roosevelt of the U.S.A.,
> You are alright with your N.R.A.
> You kept your head cool
> In the swimming pool,
> You were wise -
> Took us by surprise,
> Did not give us time to think -
> It was either swim or sink.
> But, we are with you - man, woman and child.
> Just keep up with your smile,
> Have no fear -
> You can steer
> With your hand on the sail
> The strongest gale.[6]

A man from Kentucky took the opportunity to promote his state and to reassure Roosevelt of his state's support of the NRA.

> Good tobacco, Blue grass,
> Good liqour,Fast horses,
> The prettiest women in the land,
> That's old Kentucky's stand;
> The finest state in the U.S.A.
> and mighty strong behind the N.R.A.[7]

Most of the poets played off the motto and symbol to show they understood the NRA and that they supported it. In the summer of 1933 a man from Ossining, New York, who called himself "The Nation's Poet," explained his position.

> If being a patriotic American,
> And helping every way we can;
>> In supporting the Cheif Executive,
>> And his "Industrial Recovery" plan.
> If buying from those who display the "Blue Eagle,"
>> And putting our mind and our heart:
> In the cooperation to preserve our great nation,
>> Then, we do our part.[8]

A man from San Francisco believed the country needed a boost to remain strong for the NRA. He wrote a "pep song" for it set to the tune of "Happy Days Are Here Again."

> N.R.A. is here to stay
> And we will all get reall good pay
> With F.D.R. we all will play
> Happy Days are here to stay
>
> Join the force and shout it loud
> Blue Eagle took away the cloud
> Our Banners flying at full mast
> Happy Days are here at last.[9]

For many people the NRA clearly was working. Whether this was actually true may well be debatable, but they did believe it. Their judgment of its success may have been because they saw people working again after being unemployed for so long. A woman from Massachusetts said we were on our way because of the NRA.

> On our way, night and day, doing our part for the N.R.A.
> Going in, for new deals; coming out, for true deals,
> With a code for work and play;
> That own folks, old home folks, with sad hearts, may be gay.
> Pack the old, blue depression, in a thimble,
> View the new, blue eagle, symbol,
> On our way, night and day, for the N.R.A.[10]

A poet from Nashville, Tennessee, compared Roosevelt and Hoover to physicians, one good and one not so good.

> Dr. Roosevelt appeared on the scene,
> Told his nurse standing by to be absolutely quiet,
> These cases are very, very serious
> I must change their diet
> Needing a real Doctor badly
> "Big Biz" rushed up at once
> Crying, "Give us some medicine quick
> For Dr. Hoover had played the dunce.
> Then Dr. F.D.R. vaccinated businees
> With his new medicine, N.R.A.
> Which started the factory wheels a humming
> Toward a fairer and brighter day.[11]

The NRA brought jobs for those needing them. All people might not agree, but a woman from Los Angeles had no doubt about its benefit.

> President Roosevelt is a great man,
>     For there is no better in the land.
> He founded the N.R.A.,
>     Which brought pay
> To thousands of jobless
>     And to the hearts of their wives rest
> For President Roosevelt is a great man,
>     And there is no better in the lan.[12]

In addition to bringing work to the unemployed, the NRA brought an end to child labor. It also guaranteed union rights to workers, according to a poet from Oklahoma City.

The children in the factory,
They worked from morn till night--
Child labor made the millionaires,
N R A stopped this blight;
The cotton mills made this complaint:
"To freedom,this a blow;"
Shall little children toil all night?
The NEW DEAL still says "NO."

The laboring men have asked the right
That they might organize;
Employers have still refused
Or even recognized
That laboring men have any rights
To bargain here below:
Shall we refuse them justice now?
The New Deal still says "NO".[13]

Early in the life of the NRA a man from New York state saw the hope of the program. To increase its popularity, he compared the NRA to a baseball team.

Many now are smiling as they increase their step.
Good times are coming which gives us lots of pep.
A marvellous transformation can be seen on every hand,
We have a N.R.A. Ball Club that represents the land.

Washington is the diamond,the states the outer field,
March 4th the game began,when the contract was sealed.
President Roosevelt, the new manager, tossed out the ball,
Directing quick action for the team to win by Fall.

We must do our part in the national game,
We are so in earnest,no one stops for rain.
When the game is over, then we've earned a rest,
Winning all before us by our N.R.A. best.[14]

A man from Detroit saw the NRA as the only thing needed to restore prosperity.

All aboard the good ship Nira
Sail with us to Prosperity's Shore

Leaving the twins, Despair and Depression
Bidding farewell to a thousand woes.[15]

For a poet from Georgia, the NRA was the answer to the unemploy-
ment problem. With the industrial codes, collective bargaining, and
Roosevelt's leadership, people would work again.

President Roosevelt is our friend I really must say.
He put us to work under the NRA
Times have come and times have past
But we have found our friend at last.
He is our friend truly indeed.
He will help us when we are in need.
Times are better, I really must say,
Since we are working under the NRA.
Now we are under the brand new code,
President Roosevelt will lighten our load.
He is the very best man in the U.S.A.
NOW WE ARE WORKING UNDER THE NRA.[16]

The NRA, despite the supporting poems, was not universally popular.
Many people believed it was over-regulating business, while some
liberals were concerned that the hard-won antitrust laws were being
abandoned. For whatever reason, many opposed the NRA and the
opposition occasionally surfaced in the form of poetry, most of it in the
form of ridicule. Little poetry critical of the NRA appears in the records
of the Roosevelt administration. Most of these poems are in the Hoover
Library and were sent to the former president to show him he was right
all along, to encourage him to run again, and to boost his morale.

One of the poets from Youngstown, Ohio, said he could see no
difference since Roosevelt became president.

I really do not see no change,
Sence Roosevelt took the reins,
And started what he called the N.R.A.
For the banks still print our money,
And we do not have no milk or honey,
And we will all land in the poor house, some sad day.[17]

Although it became more widespread later, criticism of the NRA
surfaced early. It was serious enough that a poet from Tennessee who
identified himself as "a Southern colored boy" sent a poem to Roosevelt

in October 1933 urging people to support the NRA and to stop criticizing it.

> Mr. patriotic Citizen of the U.S.A.
>     The President needs your cooperation with his N.R.A.
> Until relief, which is sure to come, without long delay,
>     Will be through your standing by the surest way.
>
> Though there may be times when you fell dismayed.
>     A bit discouraged, and I guess, afraid.
> But discard your pessimism, and inject optimism.
>     Above all things, cut out <u>darned</u> cirticism.
>
> The numerous codes, will hold secure,
>     Everlasting prosperityfor American's future.
> Then, why hesitate of a worthy cause today.
>     When your cooperation is demanded by the N.R.A.
>
> We must have confidence in the things which are backed,
>     By the President's great National Recovery Act.
> If we would chase this greatest depression away,
>     Then we're bound to stand by the N.R.A.
>
> We've the biggest problem of our day.
>     So wake up Mr. Citizen, you cannot betray,
> The Blue Eagle, with it's lives so gay.
>     Which is the emblem of the N.R.A.[18]

The opposition and criticism continued, however. A poet from California tried to be clever while implying that the NRA might even be subversive.

> When the brand new ship Newdealavich
> Started out from shore,
> A bird was aboard, the like of which
> Had never been seen before.
> Blue were its feathers, piercing its eyes,
> Its claws like electrical sprays.
> It gazed at the stars
> From the rigging and spars
> And no one could fathom its ways.

The skipper said to himself in his muse,
"If this bird e're gains any fame,
If it rides with me each day as I cruise,
It must have an earcatching name."
Spoke sad sailor Tony
From the land of belogny,
"To the bird without mamma or sire-a
I give for a name-a to this little dame-a
The beautiful name-a of Nira."[19]

The critics of the NRA focused on the director, Hugh Johnson, and Roosevelt. According to one poet, Johnson was determined to destroy business.

Then came the cavalry, Johnson at their head
Brandishing their N.R.A.'s till Business bled,
With a Blue Eagle sitting on each spear,
Filling all the watchers with unholy fear;
Roaring up the avenue, shouting as they came,
Putting the Night Riders evermore to shame.
With them came their victims, walking in the road,
Business men and merchants, shackled to a code
Grocerymen in abject fear, oil men in chains,
Barbers and laundrymen, and men who clean the drains! -[20]

In a parody of the famous poem "The Night Before Christmas," a poet from Cincinnati, Ohio, compared Roosevelt to St. Nick and federal programs, including the NRA and TVA (Tennessee Valley Authority), to Santa's reindeer.

With a foxy old Driver, so lively and slick
I knew in a second 't was only old Nick;
And swift as the light were ideas born but to maim,
And he bellowed and shouted, and called them by name, --
Now Nira! Now Nira! Now Tiva! Now Tiva! (NRA;TVA.)[21]

Opposition to the NRA continued to mount and it eventually found itself before the Supreme Court. When the court declared the NRA unconstitutional, a New Yorker was especially pleased and praised the court for doing its duty.

Fly out blue eagle, go today--
   As tyrant now, you do not sway--
But as old bird, you can now free
   Us from all New Deal tyranny.

Thank God for wise men holding fort--
   "Forgotten men" -- our Supreme Court--
Have looked ahead a thousand years
   And put to rest a lot of fears.

. . . . . . . . . . . . . . . . .
Thank God for bird and court and law,
   Which socked all tyrants on the jaw,
And gives a chance for men to climb,
   Set free from politics and crime.[22]

Although the NRA did not succeed as its supporters had hoped, and Roosevelt was not as upset as he appeared when it was overturned, the situation was different in the agricultural segment of the economy. Farmers had been suffering throughout the 1920s, a time of supposed prosperity. In the latter years of the decade, the plight was recognized, but little had been done to attempt to restore prosperity to farmers.

During the Coolidge years Congress acknowledged for the first time that the real problem for farmers was overproduction. Surpluses in basic commodities continued to pile up and prices went down.

Beginning in 1924 Congress debated what became known as the McNary-Haugen bill. It was passed twice, in 1927 and 1928, but was vetoed each time by President Coolidge. It was an elaborate scheme for the government to buy surpluses and sell them on the world markets at prevailing prices. Government losses were to be made up by a tax or "equalization fee" on the producers. Coolidge objected on the grounds that it was a price-fixing scheme, benefited special groups, and would lead to more overproduction.

After Hoover became president and the depression worsened, he signed the Agricultural Marketing Act in 1931. It eliminated some features of McNary-Haugen but enacted some of its basic principles. A bank examiner in Minnesota could not resist sending a poem to Roosevelt during the campaign of 1932 in which he said that if McNary-Haugen had been enacted instead of the Agricultural Marketing Act the depression could have been averted. He delighted in sending a copy of a poem that had been published in a St. Paul, Minnesota, newspaper shortly after the Agricultural Marketing Act was passed. The poet marveled at the many lives of McNary-Haugen.

Hello, there Bill, where have you been?
No one's seen you since way back when
Cal Coolidge signed your death decree
And made incisions 'round your fee,
While Jardine stabbed you in the heart
And Hoover tore you all apart.
For years we've thought that you were dead,
And here you are, revived instead.

The kittens have nine lives they say,
But you beat kittens any day.
Cal drowned you twice, we call to mind,
And went back home. You tagged behind.
The coroner's complete inspection
Revealed you died in an election.
But here you are, back big as life,
Safe through ten years of storm and strife.

Your life's been full of woes and pains,
A dozen times o'er your remains,
Your friends have said their benedictions,
But you defy all safe predictions.
Your resurrection's past belief,
A true "immortal" farm relief.
A dozen deaths don't seem to kill
The old McNary-Haugen Bill.[23]

The agrarian myth was still strong in America. Originating in the colonial period and articulated by Thomas Jefferson, many people still believed that agriculture and farmers were the backbone of America. William Jennings Bryan had said it eloquently in his "Cross of Gold" speech in 1896 and many people still echoed his sentiments. A man in Santa Cruz, California, summed up this feeling in a poem to Roosevelt, but he was not as eloquent as Jefferson or Bryan.

Hail to the Farmers who first built the Home,
With Families as unit of the Clan,
The Tribe, the State, the Nation and the Empires,
Through all the Golden Ages of the world.

Hail Agriculture then, and sing its Praise,
As Founder of the Home and Family,

The central arch of all Prosperity,
The keystone to the Progress of Mankind.
. . . . . . . . . . . . . . . . . . . . . .
And Agriculture still remains the first,
And supreme task of life, the bottom rock
Sustaining all the rest. So it should be
The first and chiefest care of Government,
AS BASE OF ALL OUR CIVILIZATION.[24]

With that kind of feeling held widely, people became concerned when farmers suffered. The conditions of people on the land in the 1930s are well known. Some of the farmers tried to explain it in verse. A man from Hope, Arkansas, said it this way.

Cotton was cheap; in fact, 'way down,
Selling evewhere for a nickle a pound.

The farmer was working and breaking his back,
Picking <u>five-cent</u> cotton and dragging <u>a</u> sack.[25]

A fourteen-year-old boy from southeastern Colorado described conditions during the great dust storms of the 1930s that became known as the "Dust Bowl."

When we came out here to the golden west,
We rattled our money and felt the best.
Wheat and corn they both grew fine,
Pumpkin and squash grew large on the vine.

But at last here came the old sand storm;
It blew out our wheat, and ruined our corn.
The grass is covered up and the well went dry.
It killed our horses and our cows did die.

The machinery we bought and couldn't pay,
Then came the collectors and carried them away.
There's nothing left but grief and woe;
We can't stay here and we have no money to go.[26]

A poet from Oklahoma City explained as a part of a long poem how important the farmer was.

The farmer always fed the world,
He only asks his rights;
His products' prices now restored--
He's worked with all his might;
His family working in the field
To reap what he might sow;
Desert the man who feeds the world?
The NEW DEAL still says "NO".[27]

When Roosevelt became president in 1933 he knew how bad the agricultural situation was. He moved quickly and during the Hundred Days session of Congress, among the numerous laws passed was the Agricultural Adjustment Act that created the Agricultural Adjustment Administration (AAA). This law incorporated many of the ideas that circulated in the 1920s. The program was designed to reduce surpluses, but its early actions in this regard caused some of its most serious public-relations problems. In some instances the government bought farm animals and killed them. The outcry could be heard everywhere. This may have been poor planning, but the AAA did begin to bring results. Farm income began to rise and farmers gained a small measure of stability.

The AAA was a popular program for many. The poets added their voices in support. An Iowa farmer was proud of the AAA and Roosevelt, but he was just as proud of Iowa's native son, Secretary of Agriculture Henry Wallace.

In think the President and Wallace are
    the greatest friends we framers ever had,
They give us triple A which by far
    Our best law and it makes us very glad
For now we know we have a living wage.
    The ten cent corn and two cent hogs are gone
with wheat and cotton on the profit page
    We now can buy, and pass the good things on
Had we not had the triple A last year
    Ten million hogs and cattle would have died
On farms a total loss with meat so dear
    To most of us it would have been denied
Our President God bless him saved this meat
    And give it to the hungry poor to eat.[28]

A man from California was also proud of them.

HAIL ROOSEVELT, AND HAIL WALLACE AS THE SAVIORS
OF AGRICULTURE IN ITS DARKEST DAYS,
WHO GAVE A NATIONAL SOLUTION TO
A MIGHTY PROBLEM NATIONAL IN SCOPE,
BRINGING THE CITY AND THE FARM TOGETHER,
WHO MADE A NEW AGE FOR THE FARM AND FARMING,
BASED ON COOPERATION AND GOOD WILL,
WHERE ANARCHY PREVAILED BEFORE, AND CHAOS
REIGNED IN AN INDIVIDUALISTIC GROUP,
THAT COULD NOT PLAN, AND NEVER COULD UNITE,
A FEAT HISTORIC IN ITS STATESMANSHIP ![29]

A Georgia resident was quite distressed that Governor Gene Talmadge did not support the AAA. His poem said that Talmadge was a traitor to the people of Georgia and it was obvious why everyone should support the AAA.

He cusses out the President,
And says the A.A.A. is rotten,
Yet the farmer gets 8 cents for his hogs
And 12 cents for his cotton.[30]

An eighth-grade boy from Montana believed Roosevelt was doing the right thing for farmers. He wrote the poem praising the president and said in the cover letter that he would like to sell the poem and use the proceeds to go to high school. Two verses from it tell how the AAA helps farmers.

He's trying to help the people
Of the good old U.S.A.
He's trying to raise the prices
Of corn, wheat and hay.
. . . . . . . . . . . . .
He is lending money
To farmers of our land.
He's trying to help the farming
Just as much as he can.[31]

A woman from Georgia tried to counter the critics of Roosevelt and the AAA.

He is back of the AAA,
He'll make the old farm pay,
He'll straighten out our land
If we'll only back his plans![32]

The critics of the AAA existed in large numbers and court challenges to the law soon appeared. Not many of the critics voiced their opposition in verse, but there were some. One of them seemed to sum up the objections in a single poem sent to former President Hoover.

Awhile ago we were not slack
    To boast the freest land on Earth
But now, to make such foolish crack,
    Arouses most unholy mirth.

I used to raise a garden crop,
    To help to pay for youngster's duds.
But now they tell me that must stop.
    I aint to sell no extra spuds.

They made the farmers slaughter sows,
    And use them only for manure.
By law the cotton grower plows
    A third beneath the ground for sure.

And then they turn around and pay
    The farmers not to do no work,
But loaf and run their cars all day,
    Instead of raising wheat and pork.

I aint much eddication got,
    Am none too handy with a pen,
Yet somehow think we have a lot
    Of ornery bughouse Congressmen.[33]

One supporter from Wyoming said the opponents were hypocrites because they complained but took government money anyway.

They hate the three A's
Call the three C's blue Jays
They grumble from dark to dawn

They take every dime
And have a good time
And say there's been no depression.[34]

In early January 1936 the Supreme Court declared the AAA uncon-
stitutional in the case of *U.S.* v. *Butler*. The court concluded that the tax
included in the program was unconstitutional and therefore the whole
law was invalid. If Roosevelt secretly might have been pleased that the
NRA was overturned because the Supreme Court killed a program
without his having to admit failure, in this case he was truly outraged.
The poets were displeased, but they were a bit more philosophical.

During the court's hearing on the law, Justice McReynolds, an arch-
foe of the New Deal, asked if it were true that farmers bought silk
stockings and woolen overcoats.[35] This so outraged a man from Missouri
that he wrote a song that he entitled "The Farmer Objects, Your Honor!"
The two verses express his feelings.

We're back to rights of states, individual,
For that's constitutional.
Yes, by gosh!
United we stood, but because we were farmers,
Oh it wasn't constitutional,
No, by gosh!

"Is it true," said the justice
"that you wear woolen overcoats?"
Why, that ain't constitutional.
No, by gosh"!
"And your wife wears silk hose when she goes out to meetings?"
"Why that ain't constitutional.
No, by gosh!"[36]

Others tried to console the president and to encourage him to
continue his good work. A woman from Iowa told him not to worry.

But how they can hurt you, we cannot see,
When you have been all that you promised to be.
They can kill the Triple A, pass the Bonus Bill too,
But there is one thing, "Dear Franklin", that can't do,
Kill the "love" that the people have for you.[37]

A Californian said the court was wrong and implied that the justices were a threat to democracy.

> Roosevelt showed the way to Agriculture
> To bring about Good Times among the Farmers.
> And these great Principles and these Ideals
> Can never die in spite of Supreme Courts,
> Who'd push aside the Welfare of the People,
> To make a Legal Phrase omnipotent,
> Controlling Destiny by Court Decree,
> SOMETHING THAT'S ALIEN TO DEMOCRACY.[38]

A man from Ohio was convinced that Roosevelt was not finished. Maybe he had another trick or two that would thwart the court.

> UNCONSTITUTIONAL THE SUPREME COURT DOTH SAY,
> IS THAT NEW DEAL-FARMER'S ACT CALLED THE AAA,
> BUT FDR'L HAVE SOMETHING IN ITS PLACE I'LL SAY,
> SO E'EN THE COURT WILL BE OUTSMARTED.[39]

One of the most popular—and many consider successful—New Deal programs was the Civilian Conservation Corp (CCC). It was initiated at the beginning of the New Deal to put young men to work. Boys and young men from the cities were employed to work on public works projects, many of them in national parks and forests. They were paid $30.00 per month; $25.00 was sent home to help destitute families and each corps member was allowed to keep $5.00 per month for pocket money. All of their basic needs were taken care of in the military-style camps where they lived.

From the beginning the CCC was a popular program that often was romanticized by participants as well as those on the outside. The large amount of poetry in the files attests to how it was viewed. Most of the poems were laudatory in nature. Some of them explained how young men were adrift before the CCC came along. Four verses from a long handwritten poem from a woman in Wisconsin said it as well as any:

> We were the Legions of Unwanted Youth,
> The Youth for whom the world could find no place;
> We knocked long at opportunity's door;
> It opened--to slam us in the face.

We wandered and brooded and tried to think;
Someway and somehow we'd get thru the days.
It wasn't much wonder some of us slipped,
For this old world was one hell of a place.

Our youth and strength a drug on the market,
Nobody needed us! Nothing to do!
Unwanted youth! Eating unearned bread!
Maybe you think it's not hell to go thru!

Then a ray of sunshine thru the dark clouds,
In our impenetrable walls, wide flung doors!
A place for us! Work for our hands! Thank God--
And Roosevelt--for the Conservation Corps.[40]

A crudely hand-lettered poem from a woman in Akron, Ohio, said it in another way:

Mr. Roosevelt Mr. Roosevelt we are surly proud of you
You took our boys from the street, you gave them something to
    do.
You sent our boys to farms, and C.C.C. camps
You saved all from being tramps
Mr Roosevelt Mr Roosevelt we are surly proud of you.[41]

Most of the CCC poems did not emphasize or spend much time talking about the conditions that made the program necessary. Instead they emphasized the value of the CCC. According to a woman from California:

An oasis in the desert,
Are the camps of C.C.C.
Work, instead of water,
In abundance you can see.[42]

Two boys from the Chicago Home for Jewish Orphans said:

A Roosevelt camp will pay your way,
By giving you all a dollar a day
For doing work, in forests, and say,
You should be happy during your stay.[43]

CCC camps did needed work in forests and other public projects, but they also provided training and education for the young men who enlisted. According to a young man from South Carolina who identified himself as "colored," the camps benefited the residents in many ways:

> Thousands of enlisted boys,
> Are thankful and happy as can be,
> For the hours that traning employs
> In camps of the CCC.
>
> Honesty, honor, truth and right,
> "Find Your Vocation" - the motto be,
> Are the "pointers" brought to sight
> In camps of the CCC.
>
> Self-reliance, self-control, other fundamentals too,
> Are taught thoroughly as can be,
> To thousands depending now on you,
> In camps of the CCC.[44]

According to the boys, they were proud to be where they were. The men from the camp near Deadwood, South Dakota, said:

> We are the members of the C.C.C.'s.
> Sleeping every night among the tall pine trees
> We feel like working for the full, full, time
> It sure beats "Brother can you spare a dime?!
>
> We are the members of the C.C.C.'s.
> Healthy, happy army of the employee's!
> No more loafing or a' hunting for a job
> Roosevelt Plan has worked, By gob![45]

Perhaps the ultimate CCC poem was written by a young man in Virginia that contained some eighty-six verses. He discussed virtually everything that went on the camps. Some of the verses are silly and contrived; he clearly was trying to write as much as he could about his experiences.[46]

A major objective, as stated earlier, of the CCC was to aid parents who remained at home. The $25.00 sent home each month did go far to provide relief to the urban poor. The words of a poem from a young man in Waterbury, Vermont, may have given the CCC more credit for success that even its strongest supporters would have considered.

> When mother's get our check
> See old daddy stretch his neck
> Little brother Johnnie jumps with glee
> Our sister's went to college
> But we get all our knowledge
> In the good ole three C.C.'s.[47]

Or as another man in a camp said:

> So when your length of time is out
> You'll go back home with fame,
> You won while in the CCC Camp
> And be worth twice your name.[48]

Another New Deal agency that was much more controversial was the WPA—the Works Progress Administration. Through the hindsight of history there is less agreement about whether the WPA was a successful program, but for most of the persons who were aided by it, there was little doubt about its success.

Where the CCC provided direct relief only to the young, the WPA assisted all types of persons. Some of the poems about the WPA discussed the conditions under which the people lived before government relief was available. For example, an elderly prospector in Las Vegas, Nevada, wrote:

> For six long years, Depression
>   Held us in fond embrace,
> It had us nearly naked--
>   The world ashamed to face.[49]

Similarly, a farmer from the high plains of Colorado who was suffering from the drought and dust-bowl conditions, not to mention excessive agricultural debt, said it this way:

> Everything we start is a failure now;
> We have no horses and we have no cow.
> We don't know what to do and we don't know what to say.
> We're all depending on the W.P.A.[50]

A woman from North Carolina was quite happy to be working on the WPA.

> The days were long, and the sun was hot -
> I walked, and walked, for a job I sought.
> I finally came to my end,
> And not a single cent to spend.
> My family needed clothes and something to eat,
> But I could not go on direct relief.
> So I went to the W.P.A.,
> And now I work and eat every day.[51]

An Arkansas woman believed the WPA had been her salvation:

> When misfortune came to me,
> I cried, "Oh Lord! how could it be,
> That from our government, I must be fed."
> Now I can truly understand the problems in our President's hands
> The problems in our President's hands,
> Because I am a happy W.P.A. worker today.[52]

The WPA was different from most relief agencies in that it provided relief to all kinds of people and it tried to give them work in the kinds of jobs they had before. Because it provided work for artists, musicians, actors and playwrights, and others doing their own kind of work the WPA was criticized as wasting public money. One musician in New York City who was receiving support was certain that the WPA was good. She said, "W.P.A. to me is a great hospital and while all of my ills are not cured, I most certainly feel that I have progressed and profited with the fit as well as the misfits."[53] She sent Roosevelt a song (complete with sheet music) she had written entitled "The Meaning of W.P.A." The song was a feeble effort to use the initials WPA in various ways such as "Work! Pull America," "Wheel Progress Along," "Walk Proud America," and "Woo Peace, America."[54] When one reads this song, it would be easy to agree with the critics that the WPA may have supported people with little talent.

The critics of the New Deal focused on the WPA because it was so visible, spent so much money, and seemed to be quite wasteful. The fact that WPA supported the arts seemed to be frivolous to many, but the critics also were concerned that persons doing manual labor seemed not to be doing a full day's work. Many critics looked upon WPA workers as

men who leaned on their shovels all day. Some said the WPA really
meant "We Piddle Around." The people who wrote to Roosevelt did not
like what was being said and praised the WPA as saving them from
despair.

One woman from Oklahoma expressed her opinion about the critics
in a handwritten poem to Roosevelt:

> Why pick on the poor W.P.A. workers
> And tell such awful dreadful things
> They may all be angles instead of shirkers
> They may all join in with the angles to sing.
> They are none of them beggars no not by half
> They all work for the money they all recieve.
> And they are so jolly they will make you laugh
> And the remarks people makes do not believe.[55]

A man from St. Joseph, Missouri, said that people should not pay
attention to Republican critics because they had a poverty of ideas.

> What would happen to the poor man of today
> If it wasn't for the W.P.A.
> The Republicans all yelp
> Cause the poor man's getting help.
> What would happen to
> The poor man today.
> The other day I heard a Business man say,
> If he was on the W.P.A.
> When they gave him his pay,
> For shame he'd turn away.
> But there are no such people of today.
> . . . . . . . . . . . . . . . . . . . .
> The W.P.A. has kept Down wars and strife
> It has saved a many a poor man's life.
> If there was no W.P.A.
> The poor man would be starving today.[56]

By the controversial third-term election of 1940, the popularity of the
WPA was waning. Prosperity was returning and the critics became more
vocal. A man from Arkansas believed that the country had not
appreciated the real value of the WPA. He was especially critical of
Wendell Willkie, the Republican nominee for president.

But now it seems that the masses have forgotten, the good deeds
   of this man,
   When along comes a BACK-SLIDER, a man who will not stand;
For the true principals of Democracy or the common man,
   He stomps and raves about the extravigance of the W.P.A.
Yet he has nothing to offer the masses in this our trying day.[57]

Despite the criticism, most of the poets were singing the praises of
the WPA and Franklin Roosevelt for creating it. The president of
Pineland College in South Carolina wrote a poem that summarized
feelings very well.

Throughout the states it has been a blessing.
It aids the best causes without uncertain guessing.
It has been Roosevelt's very heart-throb.
This W.P.A. blesses the unfortunate with a job.

The humble have been lifted from the breadline in the street,
And put on equality basis with something to eat.
The weak have grown stronger their courage to regain.
This WPA is as life-building as a refreshing rain.

It has been an up-lifter of the whole wide nation.
New buildings and streets have sprung into creation.
It has put our standards on a higher level.
This WPA has been something in which to revel.

The highways have been beautified and made secure.
The parks have been made places of retreat for the poor.
It has caused a new up-growth of trees and flowers.
This WPA could stand for wonderful powers.[58]

Despite those who justified the WPA on philosophical or humani-
tarian grounds, the average person who was now working saw it from a
personal perspective. A man from Chicago wrote a song which ex-
pressed this happiness and pleasure very well. The song had four verses
that were virtually meaningless since his major goal was for the words to
rhyme, but the chorus really expressed the joy that most workers on the
WPA felt.

Hey, hey, hey, When you coming over,
Hey, hey, hey, My next pay day

I'm just as happy as I can be
I got twenty seven fifty coming to me;
Twenty seven fifty coming to me.[59]

Other agencies of the New Deal were the subject of poetry, but few, if any, of them received the attention of the ones just discussed. One agency that was very controversial did receive attention from the poets, but not as much as one might expect. That was the Tennessee Valley Authority (TVA). The concept of a system of dams on the Tennessee River goes back at least to the time of the First World War. It was designed to control flooding on the Tennessee, a wild river by all standards, and to provide recreational facilities for residents of the region. The most controversial feature, however, was that TVA produced electric power in competition with private industry.

The most vocal critics hoped that the Supreme Court would rule it unconstitutional as it did the NRA and the first AAA, but that was not to be. By the time the TVA reached the Court, the membership was beginning to change and the struggle between Roosevelt and the Court had made the older members more sensitive to the political ramifications of their decisions.

One of the poets gave credit to Woodrow Wilson for his dream of progress in the Tennessee Valley but acknowledged that the program had to wait for a better leader.

> Along the banks of the Tennessee,
> There is cheerful Anticipation;
> Citicens - telling each other with glee:
> "Our Dream nears Realization!"
> Where Wilson has foreseen vast blessings for man,
> Where he has build his magnificent span,
> The Dam - to harness the River;
> Where envy and greed frustrated progress,
> Dooming the great works to idleness,
> Awaiting a better Lawgiver![60]

Mixed in with praise for Roosevelt, this poem also shows the excitement the people felt for the changes that were coming.

> So many the oil of patience did burn,
> During tedious years of waiting;
> At last, the wheels are beginning to turn,
> I can feel the machines vibrating.

The roaring furnace, the blast of the flame,
After all the suspense, at last it came,
The hum and the burr of the wheels;
It sounds like beautiful melody,
I'd wish to compose a symphony,
To let you know how it feels.

I'm longing to paint a picture, my dears,
A likeness in verse and rhyme;
Relieving after all these idlesome years,
Inspiring is action - sublime!
The hustle and bustle of industry
Is stirring profoundly the fantasy,
Takes it soaring to lofty hight;
It opens bright vistas of future days,
Of developements in yet unknown ways,
A vision of cheer and light![61]

A man from Memphis, Tennessee, summed up the problems in the river's valley in a few lines.

Our Country was in great distress,
Leaders done all they could do.
Many things they didn't understand
The masses were really blue

Holding Companies were getting rich,
Utility rates extremely high.
The public paid Mr. Skinner's bills
Their limit was the sky.

The people demanded justice
Exhorbant rates they couldn't pay,
So they changed the administration
And Roosevelt started the T.V.A.[62]

A poem published in the *Tennessee Market Bulletin*, the official publication of the State Department of Agriculture, emphasized the importance of electricity to the Tennessee Valley. The poem told the story of John Doe who lived in the valley and resisted the electricity brought by the TVA. He was stubborn and would not follow his neighbors.

The TVA strung brand-new wires
    O'er Johnnie's native soil,
But they might draw the lightning, so
    For lights, he stuck to oil.

The neighbors all had lights put in,
    With gadgets by the score,
To wash the clothes and churn the cream,
    But John cussed all the more.

Sich things will do for lazy folks
    Who sit around a-guessin',
"But me," says John, "I've got to work.
    I must keep on progressin'."[63]

So John Doe continued to live in the dark without knowledge of radio. One day he finally had to go to town where he heard a radio playing, much to his disbelief. When he heard farm market reports, he had a change of heart.

He heard the thing say, plain as day,
    "Hog prices are still climbing,
The outlook's bright, so feed 'em more,"
    And then it mentioned liming.

This put old John to thinking hard.
    Perhaps there's something in it.
And now his house is fully wired,
    With gadgets to the limit.

Mrs. Doe now has time to spare,
    With time for recreation;
As for the programs on the air,
    Oh, what a revelation!

No more does John sit 'round and cuss
About the world's condition,
For all this change, thank TVA
and FDR's ambition.[64]

Most of the praise for the TVA was mixed up with praise for Roosevelt and the New Deal. A crudely handwritten poem expressed it as well as any, despite the poor grammar and spelling.

> FDR has told us what to do
> build a Dam and then it's up to you
> The father of the T.V.A
> has ben a help in every way
> Men has worked that never worked before
> keeping the wolf away from their door
> depression has ben a bitter name
> but good times are coming back again.
> Chorus
> The TVA is here to stay
> and FDR has made it that way
> the good old days are coming back again
> and their will be work for our men
> Rah Rah Rah for the new deal
> and a boost for the repeal
> FDR has put us on the spot
> Where we can have chickens in the pot
> And we are going to celebrate the day
> When a dam is build by the T.V.A.[65]

When some feared the Supreme Court might overturn the TVA, a poet from New Jersey put the blame on the power companies and defended the government.

> Kill T.V.A., you nine old men,
> Is the Power Trusts' petition.
> Government is only for OUR help,
> Never our competition.[66]

Among those who lived in the valley, many of the poets could not say enough good about the TVA. In 1937 a woman from Chattanooga, Tennessee, told Roosevelt, "If you could just see how Tennessee has been transformed from gloom & dispair to a happy prosperous place, & especially my home town Chattanooga." She enclosed a song she had written explaining how important the TVA was to the black farmers in the area. She used a word to describe Southern blacks at the time that whites considered quite acceptable.

> The darkies in the valley are a-singing hallelujah!
> singing hallelujah all day.
> In the valley of the Tennessee, They're building a dam,
> to keep old man river away.

No more will he creep to the little cabin door,
or cover up the 'taters and the corn.
No more will he sweep the cotton fields away,
where the poor old darkies toil.
The darkies in the valley are a-singing hallelujah!
Singing hallelujah all day.
In the dynamo of Dixie they're building a dam,
to keep old man river away.
Our President, God bless him,
doing more for Dixie than any man has done before.
He is for the people, the crippled and the helpless,
the darkie and the poor.[67]

Other programs and agencies were mentioned on occasion, but the number of poems about them was not very large. Programs such as the NRA, AAA, WPA, and TVA seemed to strike a chord with average persons while the response to other programs was more sporadic.

The New Deal generated attention as no presidential administration had ever done before. Certainly a reason for that was the massive number of new government programs that poured out of Washington on an unprecedented scale. That the poets responded to them was only natural.

# 7

# Depression Uncertainties

The Great Depression brought a questioning of American values as never before. People wondered if the American experiment was over. Others questioned if capitalism had failed. Some believed America was in a state of decay and compared it to the last days of the Roman Empire.

The highly vaunted American optimism and belief in progress was severely tested. Perhaps, some believed, we had been wearing rose-colored glasses as far as the future of America was concerned. Maybe America was no different from Europe, that decadent, corrupt, and worn-out place from which so many Americans, or their ancestors, had escaped.

Maybe the rise of fascism was the "wave of the future" for America. With the economic collapse maybe it was time for America to give up this democratic experiment and place its fate in the hands of a strong man. Mussolini, after all, was doing things for Italy that might be welcome here. Mussolini was more popular in America in the 1930s than people liked to remember in the aftermath of the Second World War. Hitler was not as admired in America since he appeared to be a much more evil person, but there were some, even so, who thought the German brand of fascism might work here.[1]

Some dissidents were more enamored with the Russian experiment. During the 1920s many American intellectuals who visited Russia and witnessed the Bolshevik revolution firsthand were disillusioned and turned their back on it. There were others, however, who saw Marxism as the answer. The exact version of it may not have been foreseen, but this idea of upheaval and removal of the wealthy from power was attractive to some.

Quite a number of people—both intellectuals and average persons— saw a violent upheaval in the offing. They did not necessarily welcome it and they were not convinced that it would be beneficial. They did believe revolution was coming, and little could be done to stop it.

Truly, American opinion was as diverse as America. One looking back at the era today can find evidence to support virtually any pre-conceived idea about American opinion. The poets who sent their verses to Hoover and Roosevelt reflect this diversity of opinion.

Clearly one segment of Americans had not lost their confidence and optimism about America's future. Immediately after the stock market crash in 1929, President Hoover and people in his administration began to encourage optimism and confidence. They argued that there was no depression and the way to get over this slump was to have confidence and look to the future.

Much of the public responded favorably to Hoover's call for confidence. Most people wrote letters endorsing his plan and the editorial writers in newspapers and magazines did the same. Business organizations such as the Chamber of Commerce followed suit.[2] A few individuals responded by writing poems. A woman from New York City, for example, wrote Hoover in 1930 and enclosed a poem she thought would cheer up the country. Like so many amateur poets, she hoped to get the poem set to music and sung over the radio, and "put on the Screen in the Moving Picture Theatres . . . hoping it would cheer up the public a bit—and help them overcome their pessimistic outlook."[3]

> Let us all go ahead
> There is nothing more to dread
> GOOD TIMES ARE COMING AGAIN.
>
> And tho it may seem very slow
> Still we want the world to know
> GOOD TIMES ARE COMING AGAIN.[4]

In 1930 the National Organization of Credit Men met in convention in Dallas, Texas. This was soon after the stock market crash and the seriousness of the depression had not been felt yet, but the people concerned with debt and credit had to be nervous. The theme song sung by the conventioneers was an example of the optimism—or the attempt to build confidence—of that period.

> Let's sing-a song of hap-pi-ness
> Shout till the raf-ters ring
> Sing-a song of pros-per-ity
> Let every loyal mem-ber sing
> Smile-- believe that times are good
> And we'll make bad days--good days
> Hap-piness is all that mat-ters
> So keep it in your heart al-ways
>
> . . . . . . . . . . . . . . . .

We're the men of in-dus-try
Thir-ty thousand strong
We can build our pros-per-ity
By cheering up when things go wrong
Pas-sing clouds conceal the sun
But storms bring rain-bow hues
Show'rs are blessings good for everyone
So "Quit a-singing 'bout the blues."[5]

A man from West Virginia said it another way in 1931. He was defending Hoover from attack, but his verses are in the classic optimistic mode.

To be sure there are chronic grumblers,
Who always will find fault;
But if they had a hundred jobs,
Wouldn't work enough to buy their salt.

Let us not look sad and gloomy
At conditions in our land;
But Hunkle down and face our task
To do the very best we can.

The light will shine, relief will come,
When we quit kicking like a mule;
And pull together to help our Hoover
Bring us out of hard times hole.[6]

A man from Long Island in 1931 sent Hoover a poem printed on a card that he was passing around.

Depression has brought to this world a gift,
    To study and know that life is not to drift; but to
Accept conditions and stand up straight.
    Life is a thing that pays the freight
In all our dealings we feel the weight.
    The good and bad is on the Slate
Why decry the hand of Fate.
. . . . . . . . . . . . . . . . .
Life is a struggle we must admit
    So stand on your ground and show your grit.
To the man that delivers, will receive the gift.[7]

The major burst of confidence poetry came to Hoover during the campaign of 1932. Christopher Morley published in the *Saturday Review of Literature* an interview he had with Hoover. One of the things that Hoover mentioned was the country's need for a good poem to bolster confidence.[8] Immediately people from all over the country sent poems to Hoover, some hoping for his endorsement of them and others saying they agreed with his optimism.

From Cleveland, Ohio, came a poem from a man who said he was seventy-six years old and was paralyzed on his right side.

> Oh: America. Great America.
> A test of thy strength is begun.
> Shall thy mighty arm, thy vaunted power,
> Fade out like the setting sun?
> The eyes of the world are upon thee;
> From worried millions, in lands oer the sea.
> Oh: America, powerful America, what shall the answer be?
>
> Oh: America. Proud America.
> Gird on thy armor bright.
> Lead a floundering world thats discouraged and lost
> From darkness to safety and light.
> Raise aloft thy banner of trust and hope,
> That the uttermost world may see.
> Oh; America. God-fearing America.
> HAVE FAITH. Shall the answer be.[9]

In a similar vein a woman from Maryland sent a poem written by someone else. As she said, "Surely not a great poem—perhaps not even a very good one, yet expressive of many common-sensical, homely Truths."

> In times like these,when politicians please
>     With promises the state the load will bear,
>     We must recall our strength is never there -
> That walls make homes and that roots make trees,
> Think hard, work hard, find opportunities
>     Where there seem none, do each in equal share
>     The wall to strengthen and the corner square,
> And men and nations come through times like these.[10]

An unemployed cook in St. Louis sent a poem that he said "is'nt so Hot but you may be sure it was written from way down Deep."

> Things seem in a Turmoil
> In our good old U.S.A.
> It seems as tho Deprission
> Is here with us to stay.
>
> Lots of us are Hungry
> And without the Necessitys of Life.
> Just a battle from Day to Day
> Rewarded with only Strife.
>
> It seems when the Day is Over
> And the night has drawn near
> That our Efforts were in Vain
> As we go to bed with Fear.
>
> But we must change our View
> Try not to be down Hearted
> Then down the Road to Prosperity
> We soon shall be started.[11]

Another St. Louis resident sent a poem that was reflective of a lot of the thinking of the time. It is quoted here in full.

> When all your plans have gone awry,
> And thoughtless friends have passed you by;
> Don't sit and wring your hands and cry,
> Try Smilin' -!
>
> It doesn't pay to wear a frown,
> When fickle fortune turns you down;
> Be gay and carefree like a clown,
> Try Smilin' -!
>
> Don't let life knock you for a "loop",
> Or sniff the gas--headlines to "scoop"
> For when you're gone, who'll give a whoop-?
> Try Smilin'-!

'Tis said "a Winner never quits",
"A quitter never wins";
The chap that trouble cannot lick,
Is never short on grins;
So when you're forced by life's hard knocks,
To take the count of nine;
Get up and smile and after 'while,
You'll say, "I'm feelin' fine"-![12]

A person in Washington, D.C., responded immediately. Like so many others, this person believed Hoover would understand and agree to use the poem.

I am not waiting for typing, but sending the verses by messenger.

The Associated Press sends out pages less worth while. Give it to the wires, and use our facilities whereby a sentiment can reach the U.S.A. in a couple hours. The meter may be faulty—but if I catch your meaning, this is what you think is needed. Let's try it anyway and see what happens.[13]

This person expressed the belief, as others had, that the country was as good as it ever had been.

There's "Old Glory," has it lost a single star?
Is the Union weak or soon to disappear?
Is there any danger from within or from a-far?
That is sufficient ground to make us fear?

. . . . . . . . . . . . . . . . . . . . .
Is the soil less fertile now than it was, U.S.A.?
Cant we grow enough to feed us, U.S.A., and more?
Do we lack for shelter, hot or cold, night or day?
Can't we bear the burden of the hungry and footsore?

Look within, U.S.A. and in your state of mind,
Which has suffered by these recent painful years,
You will locate all the trouble. You will find
That no real good has vanished. Dry your tears.[14]

During this period of decline many people expressed the opinion that the country was sound because no real wealth had been lost. People were frightened and money went into hiding. When some people wanted to do something, however, that was frivolous, they seemed to be able to find the money. A magazine editor in the Rio Grande Valley of Texas published a poem in 1932 that reflected those sentiments exactly.

I know there's lots o' money here,
I've seen large rolls of "dough,"
But try and get it if you can,
You'll find the pickings slow.

Abnormal times, depressive thoughts,
The banks won't lend you money,
And yet large gobs of it are spent,
At any show that's funny.

At football, baseball, prize fights,
And that silly game of golf,
The spendthrifts find the money,
And quickly slough it off.[15]

A man from Los Angeles said we only need to be cheerful and smile.

So instead of all this blameing
    Dont you think a little cheer
Will do more good for you and I
    Than our oceans, full of beer
All we need is lots of trying
    Keep our heads up, dont look down
Put a smile upon our face's
    Wipe away that awful frown
Just remember our old Glory
    Will forever wave on high
We can whip this old depression
    All we have to do is try
So start smileing, quit all blameing
    See how jolly you can be
And before you even know it
    We will have prosperity -[16]

A Texan perhaps summed up the "stiff upper lip" attitude as much as anyone.

Lift up your head, my country,
Lift up your head and smile,
This soul-oppressing journey
Is in its last long mile.
We labor in the vineyard,
At work-bench, desk and field;
America plows her furrow,
The Earth shall increase yield.
We are back to normal values,
In every walk and class,
Be not depressed, my country,
You know, "This too will pass."[17]

After Roosevelt became president the poems expressing good cheer continued to come in. Some wrote what they considered uplifting poems to Roosevelt to try to keep him from becoming discouraged by the opposition to his programs that grew every day. Others wanted him to know his programs were working and that things were getting better all the time. Therefore, he should be cheerful because the country was proud of him. There were some also who wrote poems much as they had to Hoover just to reassure him that the depression eventually would end if everyone was optimistic.

In 1933, after some of the New Deal measures were in place, a woman from Cairo, Nebraska, sent Roosevelt a poem she titled "National Booster Song." On the margin she penciled in, "Hurrah for the N.R.A." One verse was typical of the booster sentiment.

If you don't like the waves of depression,
    Remember that sighs don't help none.
Just grab up an oar; and never get sore,
    While you help paddle back to the shore.
If you can't steer the boat any better,
    Then don't knock on the captain and crew;
If you don't want to get any wetter,
    Don't hinder; but help them get thru.[18]

In the same year a man from Ossining, New York, believed adversity was good for people.

Adversity can well be regarded,
    As "a blessing in disguise";

As obstacles become the stepping stones,
    By which we all must rise.

To be tried in the fire of adversity,
    Is to be welcomed and expected,
For not to yeild on his battlefeild,
    Is truly to be respected.

As "eternal vigilance is the price of success,"
    And right is the essence of good:
Adversity is fortune in another dress.
    And in truth must be withstood.[19]

The idea of coming out of the depression better than we were before appears again and again. The poets said we had to be strong and steer a straight course for everything to right itself eventually. A man from St. Louis said this to Roosevelt in 1935.

Although in spite of critics and fears,
The "ship of state" is bound to go through:
Victory is in the air with cheers,
For a Destiny commands the crew.

We have oftimes fought gloom at the door,
Weathered storms and safely made the grade:
We are now due again for the score,
As nation we've nev'r a failure made.

We now learn our lessons from the past,
And follow the course mapped out by Fate,
Not surrendering while life may last,
Nor resign ourselves to greed or hate.[20]

A man from West Virginia expressed the same sentiments in the same year.

How different, it soon shall be,
When all our people, beneath this tree,
Shall of its luscious fruit partake,
The fruit God gave for all peoples' sake.

> And as it was in Eden's day,
> God blesses us now, in His own way;
> By giving us, a ruler strong,
> Who shall with fervor, His will prolong.
>
> This ruler now, for his new deal,
> Is calling on us, with strong appeal,
> To work with him, and closely cling,
> That we may soon, prosperity bring.[21]

After the beginning of the New Deal, the country had experienced a slow economic recovery only to have its hopes crushed by a recession in 1937. Historians have noted that Roosevelt renewed his recovery efforts and some label this the "Second New Deal."[22] Not everyone was discouraged, however. A man in New York City wrote a song which he sent to Roosevelt. Like so many others he hoped to get the president's endorsement because "in saying a kind word for the song it will help me to interest singers to put it on the air."[23] The man was confident when he said, "It is not a literary masterpiece, but I believe it will achieve the desired results, when heard over the radio from one end of the land to the other."[24] One verse from the song is typical of the sentiments of many.

> PUT YOUR SHOULDER TO THE WHEEL, AND PUSH WITH ALL YOUR
>   MIGHT,
> SOON YOU'LL SEE THE FACT'RY CHIMNEYS, SMOKING DAY AND NIGHT,
> TAKE THE YALE LOCK OFF YOUR PURSE, AND LET YOUR DIMES STEP
>   OUT,
> MAKE YOUR MONEY GO TO WORK, AND KNOCK OUT FEAR AND DOUBT,
> EV'RYBODY CLEAR THE TRACK, AND GET THE WORKING CRAZE,
> THROW YOUR ENGINE INTO HIGH, AND SPEED TO BETTER DAYS,
> MISTER GLOOM, GET OFF THE WIRE, YOU'RE ON A BUSY LINE,
> WE'RE CALLING UP PROSPERITY, OUR FRIEND OF OLD LANG SYNE.[25]

A couple of amateur song writers from Joplin, Missouri, believed they had a song that would help end the depression. Like others, they wanted the president's endorsement, but they tried to appeal to his emotions. They said they wanted him to copyright the song and that one-half of the profits go into the fund to combat infantile paralysis, a cause dear to Roosevelt's heart. Apparently the president was not moved. The song did reflect a rising sentiment in 1938.

Old man depression has been with us long enough,
He's acted mighty rough, and made the going tough,
Now there's a diff'rent feeling, we give three big hurrahs,
Ev'rybody'd happy, happy just because.

CHORUS

Old Man Depression is going round the corner
Old Man Depression with all his grief and woe
Old Man Depression was such a mean old stormer
Down where it's warmer is where we hope he'll go.
With all our hopes a reeling, he stood by with a grin,
But thanks to some New Dealing, it's curtains now for him.
Old Man Depression is going round the corner,
Down where it's warmer where all depressions go.[26]

While confidence in the future was expressed by many, there was a note of anxiety that crept in, slowly at first and more intensely as the decade of the 1930s progressed. World War I had been a traumatic event for the entire world and in its aftermath anxiety remained. Through the 1920s the concern grew that the war had been caused by men for their own gain. Gradually many Americans became convinced that the United States had entered the war not for the lofty goals that President Woodrow Wilson had proclaimed but because of the power and influence of bankers and munitions makers.

In the 1920s a severe disillusionment—and later bitterness—set in. Many Americans were unhappy about the war and the continued instability in Europe afterwards. During the prosperous days of the 1920s many Americans lived as if there were no tomorrow during the days of prohibition and all that it spawned. Historians have speculated that the grim determination to have fun was an effort to forget the war, to make up for its sacrifices, and to be happy before another war came.

This disillusionment continued into the 1930s. Some people thought the depression might be a delayed result of the war, the problems of war debts and reparations, and the problems in Europe that seemed insoluble.

A poet from Utica, New York, told President Hoover in 1932 that World War I was the cause of the depression.

Don't blame our President; he is trying to find
A remedy for what war left behind.
If you recall when, he took the chair
After war effects had gripped us for fair;

> The whole world is suffering, not just U.S.A.
> That world war is making everyone pay.
> The rich, the poor, mowed down left and right
> In this depression -- this terrible fight.[27]

The money we loaned our allies during the war continued to be a sticking point. Because of the complexities the payment of war debts to the United States was tied to the payment of war reparations by the defeated nations to the victorious European powers. The continuing instability of the postwar German government made that quite difficult. Many Americans believed the Allies should keep their pledges to pay the United States regardless of what Germany did. In 1932 a man from Mississippi told Roosevelt, in a poem about Edouard Herriot, the defeated premier of France, that the allies should pay up, even though Hoover had declared a temporary moratorium on the payments.

> France ought to pay her honest debts
>     To America and her friend;
> Let Herriot forestall regrets,
>     France to his wisdom bow and bend.
>
> When France pays up she'll better feel,
>     And likewise England and all the rest;
> We can't believe they want to steal,
>     But rather that they'll do their best.[28]

After the moratorium, no other payments were made. The United States ultimately forgave the debts, but it did not please many Americans. Some eventually did accept it, however, such as the poet from Boston who signed himself a Greek-American.

> Look how the Dear Britons
> Have cleverly balanced their budget
> First locked the gold by the tons
> And used the debts as target.
>
> Elite French also with tricked dates
> Hold onto the Golden Custard
> Forgotten all about the debts,
> And ship us Yellow Mustard.

So in such a case like this
It is better to forgive
The war, the debts and all these
For just the sake of take and give.

And with this changed course
We'll bring back stability
Which the capital of course
Will need for new ability.[29]

In America of the 1930s, a new wave of pacifism arose. Americans had long been isolationists and a strain of pacifism had always existed. In the 1930s these feelings seemed more intense. Pacifism, isolationism, and general antiwar activity seemed to be ways to keep us from being tricked into Europe's wars again.

From the time Roosevelt became president the threat to peace was hanging over the world. Mussolini had come to power in Italy in the 1920s, Japan had attacked China, and Hitler took control of Germany in the same year Roosevelt took office. In the early 1930s the danger of war was increasing. Americans did what they thought best to keep their country out of another war. Some of the poets tried to remind Roosevelt through their verses how bad the World War I had been and hoped he would publicize their work.

A woman from Bismarck, North Dakota, in 1935 remembered the war and hoped that America could make Wilson's pledge come true. Despite her hopeful ending, she did not seem too confident.

"This is a war to end war,
Come, Buddy, you're needed."
From city, from dale,
Therefore, a soul was deeded.

It was called a war to end war!
But was it true?
Countries are murmuring,
Old customes have vanished,
Old rulers, old governments,
Have now been banished.

It was called a war to end war!
But was it true?

Hasn't Faith become trampled?
Hasn't Jealousy arose?
Hasn't the Peace of God left us?
Hasn't a nation proposed victory over man?

It was called a war to end war!
Let each nation then heed.
It <u>was</u> a war to end war,
To make PEACE the world's creed.[30]

In 1936 an Oklahoma City resident remembered how we had gone into World War I.

From Arctic to Anarctic now,
Americas at peace,
Such neighborhood is sure worth while,
Autocracy has ceased;
Alas ! The Eastern hemisphere
Would drag us in its woe,
Munition Makers urging on,
The NEW DEAL still says "NO".

Aggression and Autocracy
Would drag us into to war
And maim the flower of our youth,--
But such we all abhor;
Yet greed for gain and paltry wealth
Would justice overthrow,
Destroy all humanity,
The NEW DEAL still says "NO".[31]

Some poets tried to shock with their graphic descriptions of war. A man from New Jersey wrote Roosevelt in 1937. He said he thought Roosevelt might like his poem "knowing you to be an ardent pasifist, and being one myself." Even though he misunderstood the president's views his poem is a severe attack on war. He also told Roosevelt that the poem had won a contest sponsored by a local Newark, New Jersey, newspaper.[32] The judges must have been pacifists too. The poem is quoted in full here.

Dig up the corpses
Of the, oh so glorious dead.

Scatter their ashes over this
Chaotic world
So that those preparing
May breath in the
Sufferings of the
Already dead.

Exhume the bodies
From beneath their
Six foot blankets
Of bloody soil.
Bring out their skulls
Grinning at a world not yet
Satisfied.

Show them well fed rats
And rounded worms
Fat from feeding on
The stinking flesh
Of your son
And mine.

Show them youths
Unpracticed at the
Arts of being men,
Lying dead. Baited
By a new uniform
And a loud brass band
Playing "Over There."

Strip all glory
From the dead.
Show them
Medals fit not well
Upon a bony skeleton,
That praises sound so hollow
To ears that cannot hear.[33]

After war began in Europe on September 1, 1939, a Texan sent Roosevelt a poem reminding him about what happened in 1917 and urged him to maintain his resolve not to take America into another international conflict.

Be it wrong or right,
We did not start the fight;
Preserve our Peace and Might,

"AMERICA STAY OUT OF WAR".

Believe not every word you read,
Be-Ware of propaganda - Heed;
Silence our greatest need,

"AMERICA STAY OUT OF WAR".

Remember 1918 - What we gave,
Billions in money - an unknown grave;
For 67000 Americans - Peace did not save,

"AMERICA STAY OUT OF WAR".

Remember the last war - Debt,
It has not been paid - yet;
We're offered another bad bet,

"AMERICA STAY OUT OF WAR".

Cling to strict NEUTRALITY,
Avoid the "BRAWL ACROSS THE SEA;
Sacred is our "PEACE AND LIBERTY".

"AMERICA STAY OUT OF WAR".[34]

Throughout the 1930s the desire of Americans to stay out of a European war grew as the threat to peace there became more serious. Congress passed neutrality laws and the antiwar sentiment became more vocal. The poets seemed to react to specific events. When Hitler began his movements against other nations the poets responded.

In 1935 a fifteen-year-old girl from Los Angeles expressed the anti-war feeling well.

Voices shout it! Headlines scream it! War!
Men fight! Men kill! Men die! What for?
Soldiers fall, wounded and dying.
People run about,sneaking and spying.

What is the cause of it? War! War!
Dying soldiers shout for peace once more.
At home, mothers by the fireside wait.
Will their sons meet with this horrible fate?
A bomb bursts! A bullet finds its mark!
Blinded soldiers are left to a world that is dark.
Gases! Planes! Bombs fill the air!
Men lie dying everywhere.
All for an empty field or lot,
Some forlorn and desolate spot.
In days to come, let peace live long,
Lets have no war, for war is wrong.[35]

A woman from South Carolina expressed the sentiment in another way in 1935 and brought God into the plan.

LET THE CLARION CALL TO BATTLE
RING NO MORE, NOR LIFE-BLOOD FLOW,-
GLEAMING SWORDS BE SHEATHED FOREVER,
AND A FRIEND REPLACE EACH FOE;
WITH A FAITH IN ONE ANOTHER,
BORN OF GOD'S ETERNAL PLAN,
LET THE WHOLE WORLD BE UNITED
IN THE BROTHERHOOD OF MAN.

MAY THE HEALING IN THY PINIONS
CURE THE SINFUL LUST OF GREED,-
AND ALL NATIONS WORK TOGETHER
WHEN FROM STRIFE AND ENVY FREED;
TILL IN TRIUMPH HOSTS OF HEAVEN
AS OF OLD SHALL SING AGAIN,
GLAD HOSANNAS IN THE HIGHEST -
"PEACE ON EARTH, GOOD-WILL TOWARDS MEN!"[36]

The frustration of Americans with Europeans emerged sometimes, as in the case of a woman from New Jersey, also in 1935.

Why don't they love their neighbors and adore them?
War, war, horrible war.
Why do they have war, why do they kill, why do they, still?
Why do they fight man to man,
To take away some land.

Why don't they love their neighbors,
To understand and not to fight for some land.
. . . . . . . . . . . . . . . . . . . . . .
Why must they have war
And kill men, women and children for?
Why is human life so cheap,
Men, children and wives,
Why do they fight for a piece of land?
They fight hand to hand,
Because they don't understand.[37]

A woman from Rhode Island called on God but showed her anger
and frustration at the same time.

When the war that's universal
Is subdued with peace and quiet,
It will be for God decreed thus.
That's the end of all, all wars
For the iron that are shrapnells
For the steel that all call guns
That tear the flesh of brothers
And the breath God gave His own.

To the Glory of Almighty God
Who gives us corn, and wine
And to the Glory of the U.S.A.
Let's have no more dam'd wars.[38]

A woman from Iowa in 1935 had a plan to control the nations that
would make war.

If we would join the League there is no doubt
    An international peace could be attained
The Germans and the Japs would soon find out
    With isolation nothing could be gained.
A Boycott by the world would force them in,
    Then all the nations could combine for peace.
If any one should break his pledge smite him
    With all the terrors devils could release
Then seize his land and all mankind abstain
    From any contact with him or his kind,
Destroy the tyrants, let the people reign

And arbitrate all disputs with the mind,
The nations then could form a world police
Which would maintain an everlasting peace.[39]

Three people from Santa Barbara, California, as early as 1935, anticipated that Europe might call for America's help again, but they had an answer.

Our hearts all beat together
In our land of U.S.A.
It is here we love to wander
And 'tis here we're going to stay.
Let them fight their wars of glory
Put their shell holes where they may
It is here we love to wander
And 'tis here we're going to stay.[40]

From the time of the Munich conference in 1938 the road to war was open. American pacifists continued their activities but more Americans began to have second thoughts. Not yet, however, were most Americans willing to concede that the United States would intervene in Europe again. In 1937 a man from Cleveland, Ohio, asked why people cannot live peacefully together.

"War is Hell," so Sherman said,
Before they classed him with the dead.
It's great to be a soldier, fighting for the right.
It's Hell to be a soldier, in the thick of fight!
I'll bet the Yank's can lick the Japs, the Russian's, and the Hun.
And when it comes to Italy; they too would have to run.
But what's the use of fighting; giving blow for blow?
Why can't we all live peacefully, that's what I'd like to know!
Which should we do; turn left, or right?
God give us strength; God give us sight![41]

After the Munich conference where Hitler got what he wanted from France and England, the prime minister of Great Britain, Neville Chamberlain, became the symbol of appeasement. In 1939 an unidentified poet ridiculed him.

Have you any crises, have you any crises, to fix today?
With my umbrella, with my umbrella, I'm on my way.

With my parasol to Germany and Italy,
I can fix 'em all with my appeasement policy.
Mussolini, Hitler; Musolini, Hitler,
I treat the same.
Let 'em go on braying and I'll keep on playing
My waiting game.
We took care of Wilhelm; we'll take care of them,
When we get assurance from America
That America will pay the bill.
Have you any crises to fix today?[42]

Even before the satire one poet from New Jersey seemed to agree that peace at any price was better than war.

To have peace at any price,
With all nations any size
Drink a toast to all the Nations,
In the near and farther regions,
From the North and from the South,
Let's proclaim "Don't fight it out,"
From the East and from the West,
Let them chant for peace is best.

To have peace at any price,
Is an effort worth the prize,
All the Wars fought on this earth,
Are not worth the maimed and hurt,
Let's live in peace with all our neighbours,
Teachers and scholars and professors,
Employers, and Employees too,
To start a fight it takes but two.

To have peace at any price,
Let us strive for that great prize -
All the councellors on this earth,
Find an idea worth hearing,
To free the world of all war -
Stand as freemen at the bar,
Talk of peace at home, abroad,
And you're doing lots of good.[43]

When Hitler invaded Poland on September 1, 1939, France and England declared war on Germany. Although it was not clear yet, the world appeared poised on the brink of war again. American poets who were pacifists were not as vocal now, and even some of the antiwar people were hedging a bit on how and under what circumstances the United States would fight again. Most Americans, however, were still determined to be neutral. But there were still some opposed to all war as was the woman from upper New York state.

> We want no war-- To Hell with it.
> We're not raising cannon fodder;
> We'll not send our sons to be killed by guns,
> But we'll strive for a better tomorrow.
>
> We want no bombs-- To Hell with them,
> Why wrecks our home and cities;
> We struggled hard and labored long,
> Not to be crushed to ashes.
>
> We want no ghastly germs or gas,
> Or subs' 'neath silent seas creeping;
> Wantonly taking the lives we love,
> Our gallant ships secretly sinking.
>
> These devilish implements of war,
> Make vast wealth for financiers;
> But if they're willing to face the frey,
> We're willing to be good bankers.
>
> Let's pray that the day be not far away,
> When our City--Town or Country;
> Will ring with the Joy of Brotherhood,
> With Happiness Peace and Plenty.
>
> And we'll strive for Peace a Lasting Peace,
> Which shall nothing shall ever sever;
> We'll endeavor to live as brothers all,
> And blast all wars forever.[44]

A woman from Massachusetts, even before the invasion of Poland, tried to reason with the leaders.

> Oh, pause for awhile
> And think 'ere you act,
>     Makers of War.
> Hear the cries of the wounded and dying,
>     Makers of War!
> O'er the beat of the drums and the roar of the guns
> The tears of a million mothers come -
> Oh, whose is the victory when fighting is done?
>     Makers of War?
>
>     ----
>
> The gain is not theirs
> Whom ye send to their deaths,
>     Makers of War!
> Oh, the power and the gold, they are yours,
>     Makers of War!
> And ye make them wreaths and medals gay,
> But turn the world into Hell to pay!!!
> God grant that we learn a more righteous way,
>     Makers of War![45]

Most antiwar poets in 1939 and 1940 were concerned that the United States would be called on to help again. A woman from Hollywood, California, said America should stay out.

> Let them fight over there,
> Let them fight anywhere,
> Fight in England, In Germany, France or Spain.
> While other lands share
> In the battle's red glare,
> Our Nation will neutral remain.
> Let us shout,
> Let us cheer,
> There's no war over here;
> Let us stand by our leader in every way,
> Our comrade and friend
> Will protect and defend,
> The Peace of the U.S.A.[46]

During World War I a popular song had been "Over There" about Americans fighting in Europe. In 1940 poets and song writers were saying that would not happen again.

Over Here, we'll fight to keep our freedom,
Over Here, we'll fight for what is fair,
Over Here, we'll fight to keep out isms,
But will never fight over there
Over Here, we'll gladly give our life's blood
To defend the land we love so dear
Over Here, we'll fight to keep our honor
But we'll never fight over there
We will build our defense
To withhold all attempts
We will unify the western hemisphere
And our boys will be, well prepared and free
To protect our democracy.
And we all should be,
Proud that we are free,
And we'll keep our boys Over Here.[47]

Another songwriter said Americans would stay home, but she was clearly concerned about invasion or subversion in America.

We won't go over there, no we won't go over there;
We'll help in any other way, But we won't go over there;
Now listen, Mister Hitler and Mister Stalin, hear
We'll teach you both a lesson. If you try to come over here.
We are a peaceful country and a great Democracy
But we'll fight to the last man, if you dare just come and see-

Wake up, Americans, wake up!
Wake up and drive the traitors out
We have no room for rats
In this our native land
So wake up and drive the traitors out.

Now, here's some good advice to all who look our way;
You'd better look twice before you start for the good old U.S.A.
And if you think we're softies and easily pushed around
The shoe will be on the other foot. If you ever should touch our
    ground
Now listen, all you traitors, who are here within our shore
It does not pay to bite the hand of friendship any more.[48]

A man from New York said if Europe wanted to invade the United States, Americans would be ready.

```
WE NEVER LOOK FOR TROUBLE
BUT SHOULD IT COME OUR WAY
WE WILL FIGHT WITH ALL OUR MIGHT
FOR THE U.S.A.
HERE WE PROMISED TO PROTECT
COLOR, CREED OR RACE
AND DEFEND THE FLAG
ANY TIME OR ANY PLACE
LET 'EM COME, LET 'EM COME, LET 'EM COME. . .
WE'LL BE WAITING FOR THEM --- EVERY MOTHER'S SON
THEY WILL FIND US EVERYWHERE
ON THE SEA AND IN THE AIR
OUR ARMY AND OUR NAVY BRAVE BE[Y]OND COMPARE
WE WILL FIGHT FOR FREEDOM PEACE AND LIBERTY
WE WILL FOR THE WORLD DEMOCRACY
WE ARE PREPARED AND NOT AFRAID
IF THEY WANT TO INVADE
LET 'EM COME, LET 'EM COME, LET 'EM COME.[49]
```

After the invasion of Poland, American poets began to speak out in opposition to the pacifists, isolationists, and anti-war advocates. In 1939 a student from North Carolina said it was time to get ready again.

> The sound of war is in the air.
> It's heard right here at home.
> Do the oceans separate us from the airplanes that roam?
> Republicans and Democrats,
> Let's all join hands and say ---
> We realize our president's right!Re-arm the U.S.A.[50]

In 1940 a medical doctor from Brooklyn said our potential enemies should have no doubt about America's position and determination to defend itself.

> We've no place for Adolf, Benito, or Joe,
> They who desire them know where to go.
> We'll fight if needs be, in order to save
> This wonderful land for the free and the brave.
> So arise and prepare to keep what is dear,

Be ready to fight; even die without fear,
To keep the agressors far from our doors,
We'll always be ready to defend our shores.[51]

A Texan agreed that this was not a time to be timid. He said
Americans had to get behind the president.

You heard the "fire side chat" no doubt,
Heard what Roosevelt had to say,
In his last plea for aid "All Out"
To save the democratic way;
If we love Democracy
And liberty is worth a cent,
We must on one thing all agree
And rally to the President.
. . . . . . . . . . . . . .
Dark days for Europe lie ahead
And then, darker ones we'll see.
Are patriots asleep, or dead?
Will we fight to still be free?
Mussolini is on the march.
Hitler seems to be hell-bent;
By the light of Freedom's torch
Let's get behind the President![52]

In 1941 a Virginian went even further and promised American aid to
the allies even before the attack on Pearl Harbor brought America
directly into the war.

Conquered Nations, arise! and have courage now!
Our Country's aid and might is behind you -
We'll help to fight, and win, - we vow!
To our traditional LIBERTY, we will be true!

In this critical moment of the Hour
We will come bravely smiling through
And donate all our American Power,
Our invincible Air Force and Navy too!

Liberty, Justice, Equality, and "Plenty" for all
Shall be and must be the birthright of all men, -

"To liberate enslaved Mankind," shall be our goal!
So that Men may walk with dignity the earth, again.

Tyrants and Dictators, take heed!
We mean to fight, until the battle is o'er
For ours is the noblest cause, indeed -
We shall triumph as we have triumphed before![53]

America faced a crisis in the 1930s that had many facets. There was economic decline, a crisis of confidence, and a rising threat to the peace that eventually led to another world war. Many wondered what the future could hold for the American democratic experience with so many seemingly insoluble problems facing it. What would the future America be like, many wondered. Many feared civil strife—as indeed there was scattered throughout the country. But the word in the minds of many, sometimes spoken and sometimes unspoken, was revolution.

During the depression the possibility of revolution was discussed widely in intellectual circles. It was discussed in social settings and in the pages of some magazines. Among average people apparently it was not discussed very widely, but there seemed to be a foreboding that something was about to happen, especially in the early years during Hoover's administration. Most feared the thought because of what it might bring in misery and what the nation might look like afterward, but some welcomed the possibility, believing that any change would be an improvement.[54]

Today we still do not know how close the nation was to a revolution —or merely widespread civil conflict—during the depression. There has been no indepth historical study of this question, probably because the subject is so difficult to investigate. When people who lived through the depression are asked how close the country was to armed revolt, many say that it was imminent, but that the election of Roosevelt in 1932 prevented it. One is not sure if the memory of such people is an accurate gauge of opinion at the time. Some historians have reached the same tentative conclusions—that rebellion was a strong possibility but that the people gave the democratic process another chance in 1932 and elected Roosevelt.

Roosevelt, they believe, saved capitalism and American democracy. Yet the America that emerged after Roosevelt was significantly different from what it was when he was elected. To Roosevelt's enemies, the result was unfortunate. To many of them, *he* was the revolution and American was changed forever—for the worse.

Depression poets sometimes expressed their opinions about revolution. Yet, the number of poems on this subject are not as numerous as might be expected. Sometimes a poet would attack the rich, Wall Street manipulators, or others they opposed and predicted serious trouble for these people. The language often did not speak directly to revolt, but the hint of something is there.

An example of this language is the poem by a woman from Los Angeles in 1935.

> The bulldogs all are barking on Wall Street of New York.
> They are waiting for their beefsteak to add to their salted pork.
> They're ready for the portion as they were before the "Slump."
> But Franklin D. Can plainly see That the steak must be tossed
>     where it is free.
> For a bulldog's grip is hard to rip
> When the steak is caught and not fairly bought.
> Just stop your barking on Wall Street!
> We have a man who gives no treats.
> You will buy and keep your dear old steak
> At the price that he is likely to make.[55]

In 1936 a poet from Oklahoma City, in one verse of a long poem, talked about the battle with Wall Street.

> For every since the Civil War
> We've been ruled from Wall Street;
> Our Government has been returned
> To Washington--a feat---
> But only with gnashing of teeth,
> A battle with this foe;
> Shall we give up to entrenched greed?
> The NEW DEAL still says "NO".[56]

A poet from Chicago talked about how the wealthy had been brought under control and the nation had been saved.

> Those whom wealth and privilage,
> Made arrogant and strong,
> Beleive this land belongs to them,
> You told them they were wrong.

For progress will not wait,
And listen to the verbiage,
Of wavering men who'd trade our rights,
For a mess of legal pottage.

Do not those eminent sages know,
So steeped in erudition,
They must preserve the rights of men
If they'd preserve the nation.[57]

Others spoke more directly to the coming upheaval. In 1932 a man from Arizona sent a poem to Roosevelt while he was still governor of New York about the eviction of the veterans who had been in Washington demanding early payment of the bonus. He was very upset by the way the veterans had been treated. He spoke of coming violence which could have been an international enemy, but it could also have come from within.

They'll need them again,
　　Sons of the blue and gray,
And their adopted brothers
　　Who fought so gallant that day.
When another enemy
　　Will spurt gas and fire
Threaten to reduce our cities
　　To funeral pyres.

When from explosives in air
　　The dome of our capital'll sway,
They,d wished they,d granted
　　These loyal boys their pay.
When mothers with babes
　　Seek dark caves to pray
For those grim old veterans
　　To come save the day.[58]

During the campaign of 1932 a man from Chicago sent President Hoover's assistant a poem which had been published in the *All Chicago* magazine. A close reading of the poem reveals no subversive intent, but the letter writer reported that he had prosecuted the poet in 1918 and sent him to prison for activity with the Industrial Workers of the World (IWW). He laments that no investigation is underway of the IWW or communist organizations and believes a case could be made against them. Certainly the poem is critical of Hoover, but no more so than dozens of others. One wonders if the letter writer were equating criticism with communism or other, subversive activities.[59]

Often the concern about revolt or communist subversion appears incidentally in poems about other subjects. For example, a high school boy from Phoenix, Arizona, in a poem promoting optimism made a reference to communism.

> When your home is up for auction, and your jewelry's all in hock,
> And you've used up every penny from the old proverbial sock,
>> And your kids are going hungry, and their clothes are all in shreds,
>> And you've become the natural prey for communistic Reds;
> Oh, then's the time a feller must buck up and do his share
> Since he's only one of many, and it wouldn't be quite fair
>> To receive especial benefits while others are in need;
>> 'Twould be unpatriotic to show selfishness and greed.[60]

He does not hint at rebellion, but he does imply that communism is becoming more attractive to the people. A poet from West Virginia made a similar reference in a poem praising Roosevelt.

> Isn't it wonderful to know
> That capitalism will have to go;
> Such as was controlled by a few,
> Who seeking wealth, in selfishness grew.
>
> Uprooted was this powerful thing,
> Then replanted close by a spring;
> Where it could drink of waters clear,
> And spread its branches, both far and near.[61]

Some of the poets were more direct. For example, a man from Houston, Texas, said he wrote an original poem every day for the *Houston Press*. In 1935 he wrote one praising Roosevelt and condemning his critics. He began and ended the poem talking about revolution.

> We came within a scarce six months of having revolution,
> And no man raised his voice or whispered Constitution!
> We faced the silent fury of a patient mob which groped
> In utter darkness, knowing that the things for which they hoped

Would never happen, unless some great outstanding brain
Would reach forth and grasp the guiding rein
Of governing power, and check a nation in its onward flight.
Through something worse than Stygian darkness of a Doreian
 night.

. . . . . . . . . . . . . . . . . . . . . . . . .

My logic may be crude, devoid of common sense;
We faced an issue which constitution couldn't save;
We forced that issue—we conquered exigence,
And now we listen to anarchists who rail and rave.
No thanks we give to him who stopped a revolution,
Who saved for us our country and its constitution.[62]

There were a number of other poems in a similar vein. They were usually about something else and incidentally mentioned the problem. They also were usually written after the poet believed the threat had passed. A Texas poet was talking about the rich when he said:

For they shall pay your sin back double,
    And you shall vanish like a bubble,
And you shall burn like chaff and stubble,
    And never shall you cause them trouble
        Any more![63]

A man from the Bronx in 1936 recounted how things had been when Roosevelt became president.

THE Bankers were at a verge of a revolution
Not being able to keep up their institution
Most of the Human-beings without exageration
Were starving to death throughout the nation[64]

A man from Arkansas expressed similar sentiments.

When Roosevelt took command, the country was on the verge of
    revolution,
He put His noble brain to work, and soon found a solution,
For all the economic ills and wants, that troubled the nation,
Now prosperity reigns, and Roosevelt is the man for His station.[65]

Revolt and communism were considered the same thing by some poets. A woman from Los Angeles was pleased in 1938 that Roosevelt had saved the nation.

>When Technocrats, Autocrats, Aristocrats
>>Talked much on Evolution
>>>Each one striving ahead-
>>>>The homeless and hungry
>>>>>Murmered aloud "Revolution"
>>>>>>Our Star Spangled Banner
>>>>>>>Almost changed into "Red".[66]

A man from Chicago said in 1936 that we had almost become communists but that Roosevelt had saved us.

>As the man who won "THE FORGETTEN MAN'S BATTLE"---
>Of a Nation grounded in Equity,
>But which 12 wronged years enslaved it
>In the bonds of Plutocracy;

>>In a spoils-system of exploiters,
>>Foisted by the Royal Economists:
>>Princes of Privelege! of Special Licence!
>>Whom near made us Communists.[67]

Roosevelt had come along at just the right time according to a man from Massachusetts.

>The Hoover administration had been letting things slide,
>And our country was fast going down with the tide.
>The unemployment situation was certainly rife,
>And quick action was required to prevent civil strife.[68]

Not all who were concerned believed Roosevelt was the answer. A poet from Corpus Christi, Texas, believed he was the problem—that his policies were leading to revolution in 1935.

>Each new department made new laws,
>>Proved foolish by a second---
>Confusion grew, and no man yet
>>The total wreck has reckoned.

> The good plain folk are struggling on
>   In baffled evolution,
> Hope long deferred,hearts more than sick,
>   And fearing revolution.[69]

From hindsight, revolution clearly was not to be the fate of the United States. Had the depression continued unabated in 1933 without any significant attempts to resolve it, the scattered episodes of violence occurring around the country may have become more serious and more widespread. Without someone and some program to give the people hope, such as Roosevelt provided, a man—or possibly a woman—with charisma might have gained a following that could have led to a violent upheaval. Huey Long of Louisiana had a significant following before his assassination in 1935 and Father Charles Coughlin reached millions through his radio broadcasts. Neither of them seemed to be the leader who could grab the attention of the nation toward revolution, but there may have been others in the land who could have moved toward such a position had the opportunity presented itself. With Roosevelt this possibility was thwarted.

Truly the 1930s was a time of uncertainty for the nation. The people worked their way through it, but it was not an easy task. The poets of the 1930s helped to chronicle the steps and missteps of the decade.

# 8

# The Shine Tarnishes

Franklin Roosevelt generated extreme opinions. Everyone seemed to love him or to hate him. Few had moderate reactions. If one reads the letters and poems in the Roosevelt Library, it would be easy to conclude that everyone—or almost everyone—loved Roosevelt and his programs. On the other hand, an analysis of editorials might cause one to conclude that he was very unpopular. The election results show a different opinion, however. Roosevelt's reelection in 1936 was the greatest presidential victory in American history. Even in 1940, when he broke the two-term tradition and caused a storm of protest, he still won reelection handily. Again in 1944, when the resistance to a fourth term was not as great, he still won. Clearly, the majority of the people supported him enough to vote for him again and again.

George Wolfskill and John A. Hudson, in their book, *All But the People*,[1] analyzed opposition to Roosevelt and his programs. They concluded that on looking back everyone in the country seemed to hate Roosevelt. The attacks on him were so widespread and so vitriolic that Roosevelt could be considered one of the worst things to happen to the country. Everyone seemed to hate him—"all but the people"—thus the title of their book.

An analysis of the poetry and song lyrics reveals that Roosevelt did have his critics, but the percentage of critical verses is small in comparison with the praise. The patterns of praise and criticism are clear. In the beginning the praise was almost universal. During the campaign of 1932 and in the first year or two of the New Deal, most of the criticism can be found incidentally in poetry praising Hoover. As the years passed and New Deal programs increased, some people, naturally, became critical of Roosevelt. Criticism varied in intensity with various issues that arose. During Roosevelt's reelection campaign in 1936, many opponents took the opportunity to pen verses opposing him. When Roosevelt attempted to change the composition of the Supreme Court, one of the greatest controversies of his administration erupted. The breaking of the two-term tradition in 1940 was almost as controversial. In both instances, poets responded to criticize, attack, or chide the president.

**167**

Throughout the New Deal poets criticized various programs and members of the administration. Mrs. Roosevelt was quite controversial because she broke many traditions that most people expected of the First Lady. She was an activist, outspoken, and opinionated. Roosevelt liked to say that she was his legs and went places he could not go and reported to him what average people thought. She did not escape the critical poets. Neither did Roosevelt and other personalities of the New Deal.

During the campaign of 1932 there were many people who criticized Roosevelt, but few, if any of these attacks were personal. Soon after he became president in 1933 and began to take unprecedented action, the personal attacks began. They criticized his programs, but they also reminded him of his campaign promises he was violating. During the election of 1932 an unidentified poet sent a poem to Hoover that said the Democrats were talking panic too much.

> So all of this talk of a panic
> Of the country about to go "flunk"
> Between you and me and the toastmaster
> Is a lot of damn Democrat "bunk".[2]

A poet from Lancaster, New York, Roosevelt's home state, said that the New York governor was not up to the task.

> The Governor of the Empire State,
> Has had a lot to say,
> All about the Fall Election
> And the problems of the day.
> . . . . . . . . . . . . . .
> Now I'd like to ask one question,
> And I think that I am fair:
> What has Franklin D. to offer
> If elected to the Chair?
> . . . . . . . . . . . .
> Every time these men start talking,
> They are sure to tell us that
> We will all be sitting pretty
> If we'll let them go to bat.
>
> But a glance back through the records
> Will reveal things written there,
> That will prove they can't be trusted
> In the Presidential Chair.[3]

After the election, but before Roosevelt's took office, a few poets tried to console Hoover on his defeat and attacked Roosevelt in the process. For example, a woman from Massachusetts told Hoover that people voted for Roosevelt for all the wrong reasons.

> There were several million people
> Who just voted with the Mob,
> They beleived the tales of Roosevelt
> That they all would get a Job.
> . . . . . . . . . . . . . . .
> So the horde of thoughtless voters,
> Never counting up the Cost
> Turned against our valiant Leader
> And the cause of Right was lost.
>
> Yet the thinking, helpful people
> Will be staunch and kind and true,
> And will carry on like Hoover
> In whate'er there is to do.[4]

A booklet with a lengthy poem of abuse was sent to Roosevelt early in his presidency. This unidentified poet reminded Roosevelt of his promises.

> Who, in the year of '32,
> Made promises to all--to you--
> And then forgot to put them through?
>     'Twas Roosevelt.
>
> Who, on March fourth in '33
> Held up his hand and swore that he
> Our Constitution's guard would be?
>     'Twas Roosevelt.
>
> Who then went forth with haughty stride,
> Put constitutions all aside
> And chose himself our only guide?
>     'Twas Roosevelt.[5]

Another unidentified poet sent Hoover a poem with similar sentiments.

In the scarce and weary days of thirty-two
We heard your promise and battle cry, -
The blame was Hoover's and you the god
For sift and thrift and living clod.
No Debt for you, less Tax for us, all safe ahead,
Fewer Commissions, Balanced Budget, Forgotten Man.
Your words flew, we thought you knew and were wise,
And so we shifted our faith and lifted our eyes,
Although we knew the panic was worldly wide
And how could even Hoover panic other tides?
We knew your voice was good, we hoped it true,
But now we know brave truth no brake for you.
Ego actor, super big, untamed by custom or mistake,
Sad wisdom mourning and betrayed, went away.

Americans think deeply, feel finally for the inner man, -
The actor is not the man nor nimble talk, reward or scheme,
Nor spite at rival nor restless dash at space and time, -
These but fouls and wild pitches to the safer, balanced man.[6]

Another poet told Hoover in 1936 that Roosevelt had misled the people.

He promised everything men cried for;
Extolled the flag our true men died for;
Would have jobs for all applied for -
He would end the dire depression,
If he could but get possession
Of the reins of Government.
When he smiled he seemed "God sent."
Voters gave him all they had.
Now:--- Is he mad?[7]

One of the major campaign issues in 1932, other than the economy, was the future of the issue of prohibition. Roosevelt was for repeal of the Eighteenth Amendment, but not all Democrats agreed. Roosevelt did not personally make a big issue of it, but many on both sides did. Many of the Republican supporters of prohibition attacked Democrats for supporting repeal and indirectly attacked Roosevelt.

Methinks he'll strike many a problem
    When he dons the President's gear,

Will he repeal the Eighteenth Amendment
Or give only light wines and beer?[8]

During the campaign a New Yorker said prohibition was not really
the issue and Hoover would prevail.

We sing about our governors, also our wines and beer
But when it comes to staighten things we call the engineer.
So Herbert, you'll be busy for the next four years
With business and more important than dispensing wines and
beers.
So here's three cheers for Hoover, three cheers for Curtis too
For they're the boys that fear no noise and they will see us thru.[9]

Another poet said that Roosevelt picked the wrong people for the
wrong reasons. The people mentioned here are Al Smith, the Democratic
candidate in 1928, and John Nance Garner, the vice presidential
candidate in 1932.

Franklin has the queerest friends - that isn't any news:
Al has lots to say - it's mostly bigotry and booze:
Johnny's brain pan rattles for it's full of nuts and screws.
We're for Hoover now.[10]

The poet from Massachusetts mentioned earlier said Roosevelt made
promises that were wrong.

A group of men stood talking
And they answered with a sneer,
"Sure we gave our votes to Roosevelt
Now we're going to get our beer."[11]

A woman from Montana who was vice president of the local
Women's Christian Temperance Union (WCTU) chapter believed
Roosevelt and other politicians had deceived the voters on the the
prohibition issue.

Oh, shame to our nation!
One scarce could believe
How low politicians
Will stoop to deceive!
And we blush for the manhood

That bawls: "we want beer!"
When for wives and for babies
   Plain bread is too dear.

Oh, woe to our country!
   Too late some will know
That the fool vote they cast
   To a menace may grow;
When, discouraged by plodding
   Depression's foul mire,
They have leaped from the frying-pan
   Into the fire.[12]

One poet in 1936 said that Roosevelt's promises about how the end of prohibition would bring in revenue were not true.

One pledge he kept. He gave us beer.
The golden days he made so clear,
Before election, - they are not here.
The millions claimed in revenue,
From liquor taxes he would put through,
Are dreams still hoped for, over-due.
"Liquor Control!" we've never had.
Now:--- Is he mad?[13]

The opponents of Roosevelt seized any opportunity to criticize him—and he gave them many opportunities with the many new programs he initiated. When Roosevelt brought Democratic control back to Washington after twelve years, it was inevitable that many new, and unfamiliar, faces would be in the limelight. In addition to the professional politicians that one would expect, Roosevelt brought a lot of young academics and other professionals with him. One of the most controversial innovations was the so-called "brain trust." Originally called the "brains trust," this was a group of young men (mostly) who were close to Roosevelt and had influence with him. Some were in the cabinet, some were in lower-level positions, and some were in the White House. Although it was not entirely true, this group of advisors was thought to be primarily college professors. To the critics of the New Deal the brain trust appeared to be a group of unelected, idealistic, and unrealistic academics. Many of the poets resented them.

One poet told Hoover the brain trust was changing what America was all about.

Then came the priests of the famous New Deal,
Young men and old men, their eyes full of zeal,
Mortarboards and tassels on each bulging brow,
Chanting all together that "They knew how.
"down with tradition, commonsense, and custom.
"We'll run the bankers, or else we will bust 'em.
"We'll spend the money. We'll deal out credit.
We'll save the nation." and the crowd roared, "You said it."[14]

A Texan believed that these advisors were responsible for the farm program.

He called professors from their chairs
    To add their wits to his
And help his plan to save each man
    His swiftly shrinking biz.

The crack-brained crew instructed then
    The farmers not to plow,
And raised the wage of laboring men
    By raising prices--wow![15]

A man from Florida was concerned that the brain trust was foreign to American traditions and was dangerous.

He thinks he owns the White House, mistaken sure is he;
He subtly works, experimenting, trifling with liberty.
The brain trust, very clever, a foreign idea,
His politicians are worsted, his party is disgusted.
Our once great land is floundering, but not for very long;
Our patriots are seized with trembling, but listen to their song![16]

A resident of New York City longed for the old days when presidents did not have so many advisors around them. In those days presidents had time to think and make reasoned decisions. All that had changed, he believed.

When we were boys the presidents
Maintained a certain reticence
Concerning high affairs of state
Till they had time to cogitate.
They pondered deep o'er problems new

To find solutions tried and true.
The nation's wealth they never spent
On theory and experiment.
They thought again and still again
Alone. There was no "brain trust" then,
But Washington has now become
For nervous theorists a home
And there the New Deal broth they brew
As mixed as that which Macbeth knew.
Into a boiling pot they throw
All that they ever hope to know
And more, to which are added pages
Torn from the works of many sages.
At last they redden it with sparks
Out of the writings of Karl Marx.
Meanwhile to sway the public mind
Publicity of every kind
Sweeps o'er the land much like a flood
That's full of sticks and scum and mud.[17]

To some poets the brain trust was responsible for so many terrible things. To many the advisors were subversives who were turning the country in the wrong direction. In 1934 a man who called himself "A Tory" published a booklet entitled *Frankie in Wonderland*, which was a parody of *Alice in Wonderland*. He had the following to say about the brain trust.

"Taxpayers," said the Brain Trust boys
"We've had a lot of fun,
We've socialized the U.S.A.
And put it on the bum,
You can not call your soul your own,
We haven't left you one."[18]

Another poet who saw the brain trust as socialists set his poem to the tune of "Battle Hymn of the Republic."

Mine eyes have seen the crumbling
Of the corner-stone of life.
Roosevelt tramples out initiative
With his socialism rife.
He has loosed his fateful brain-trust

And there's everlasting strife,
As his plans come surging forth.[19]

A man from Illinois saw the New Deal led by the brain trust destroying American freedom.

My Country, 'tis for me.
Land of lost liberty:
F.D. I sing of thee
Land where my rights have died!
Land where professors tried
To take us for a New Deal ride
Lest freedom ring.[20]

A poem entitled "Tired" circulated widely during the New Deal. It can been seen in various forms—handwritten, typed, and printed in newspapers and magazines. Despite its being copied so many times, the words remained quite consistent. This is different from other popular poems that were changed in some respects as they passed from hand to hand. This poems contains two lines about the brain trust.

I'm tired of every new "Brain Trust" thought;
Of the Ship of State - now a pleasure yacht;[21]

One of these poems had some figures added at the end which reveals how one person viewed the New Deal programs.

SOME NEW DEAL FIGURES

| | | |
|---|---|---|
| U.S. Population (approximate) | | 120,000,000 |
| Eligible for old age pensions | 46,000,000 | |
| Children prohibited from work | 30,000,000 | |
| Government Employees | 32,000,000 | |
| Unemployed | 11,999,999 | 119,999,998 |
| | | 2* |

*Left to produce the U.S. Wealth

Just you and I and I am all worn out.[22]

Some poets singled out specific members of the brain trust to criticize. One of the most well-known, and in some ways controversial, was Harry Hopkins. A social worker by background, he was close to

Roosevelt and served in many positions. Eventually he was Roosevelt's closest foreign policy advisor who served throughout World War II. A West Virginian was not impressed with Hopkins and set his objections to verse.

> The political bum, who says we're dumb,
> Will learn that Mountaineers are free
> And refuse to take the Hopkins crumb,
> From the hands of treachery.
> . . . . . . . . . . . . . . .
> Dark chamber councils,Hark-Beware
> Iniquities in them prevail
> But for betrayal and a snare
> They failed to hide its daggy tail.
>
> "Montani-Semper Liberi,"
> The Motto we will honor most
> Inscribed on banners with the cry
> We will route for good the Hopkins host.[23]

An unidentified poet saw Hopkins as the man who was throwing away the public's money. This selection reflected the attitude of many of the opponents of the New Deal.

> Next came the bureaus, countless thousands strong.
> Headed by Hopkins; and this was their song:-
> "Can you use a dollar? Do you need Relief?
> "Come, oh ye voters, and tell us your grief.
> "We'll give you jobs, or else ready money.
> "We'll make America the land of milk and honey.
> "Get what you can from local philanthropy.
> "We'll do the rest. Your Uncle's no misanthrope."
>
> How the people cheered as Hopkins passed.
> One man sighed, "It's too good to last,
> "Some day I suppose I'll have to get a job,
> "Or loot a grocery store as part of a mob."[24]

A New Dealer often criticized was James A. Farley. He had been Roosevelt's campaign manager and was named postmaster general in return. This cabinet position often went to campaign leaders. The same poet who criticized Hopkins did not like Farley either.

Farley came first with his big bass drum
Louder than a mail-plane's twin-motored hum,
Leading the procession of the hungry and the lean
To fresh patronage where the grass is green.
Office-seekers followed, with their eyes a-blear
Pounding out the chorus on their bellies full of beer.
    "Down with the dollar
    Up with the tax.
    If you don't like it,
    You'll get the axe."[25]

Another poet, mentioned earlier, who set his poem to the tune of the "Battle Hymn of the Republic," named several other members of the brain trust as bringing the country to ruin.

With his Wallaces, his Tugwells,
His Morgenthaus and Franks
He has split us all asunder
And forced us into ranks.
Dictatorship shall follow
For the world at large to see
As his plans uncover all.[26]

Despite all the concern about the brain trust, one poet wanted people to remember who was responsible for it. The man published a long poem in a booklet entitled *Roosevelt* which had as its frontispiece the following:

Although in '32 he won,
Now, judge by all he's said and done,
PUBLIC ENEMY NO. 1
IS FRANKLIN DELANO ROOSEVELT.[27]

This poet blamed Roosevelt for the brain trust.

Who called the brain trust to his aid
To take the curses, shafts and blade,
Then coldly pushed them to the shade?
    'Twas Roosevelt.

Who chose that brain trust?--Let's be fair;
'Twas Franklin Roosevelt called them there--

Give Frank, not brain trusts, gaffs and air.
Yes, Roosevelt.[28]

Another poet from New York was hopeful that the New Deal would soon be over.

The fireside chats and blarney dies,
Professors and the "brains" depart,
Still stands our modern sacrifice,
A crushing debt, a broken mart.
Lord God of Boasts, you're with us yet,
We can't forget--We can't forget.[29]

Critics jumped at anything they thought might discredit Roosevelt. Many of them were dismayed by the many new government agencies created by the New Deal, especially by the alphabetical acronyms by which they were known. As a poet from Long Island said in 1935 in a very long poem:

And if they keep increasing more
    He'll then have some to let.
For he's used up all the letters
    In the English alphabet.[30]

A Minnesotan said the New Deal agencies were costing the public far too much money.

Be it muslin,calico,blankets or socks,
    Or strikes and unrest among the flocks,
Or a weekly donation to the idle that be,
    Or a jumbled alphabet from A to Z,
Or a bronze Plaque in History's hall,
    John Q Public pays for it all.[31]

An anonymous poet in a poem entitled "Alphabetically Speaking" used real and fictitious agencies to express his dismay.

Unless these New Deal Democrats
Stop pulling bureaus out of hats,
I fear that soon we'll have to get
a new and larger alphabet.

Now, what the country needs today
is less and less of N. R. A.,
B. U. N. K. and E. T. C.
But more and more of C. O. D.

For in the sweet, sweet bye and bye
Somebody has to P. A. Y.
For all this "Jack" the U. S. A.
Is handing out so free today.

Our star of hope is growing dim;
We'll soon be on the B. U. M.
We'll struggle, starve, and break our necks
To meet the future T. A. X.

Unless I make an N. G. Guess,
It's time to sound an S. O. S.,
And stop this flood of I. O. U.,
And I mean stop it P. D. Q.

So I beseech you F. D. R.
Don't stretch the alphabet too far.
My shirt is gone; now, mister, please
Don't take away my B. V. D.'s.[32]

A widely circulated poem said Roosevelt used the alphabetical
agencies to pacify the people.

When they started to worry,stew,and fret
I'd get them chanting the alphabet
With the A A A and the N L B
The W P A and the C C C
With these many units I got their goats
And still I crammed it down their throats[33]

Critics of the New Deal sometimes attacked members of Roosevelt's
family as a way of getting at him. Eleanor Roosevelt, the president's
wife, was a favorite target. Roosevelt's children also came in for criti-
cism. This is not so surprising at the end of the century with so many
presidential children being in the limelight and often the center of
controversy. At the time of Roosevelt's administration, however, it was a
bit unusual. Their daughter obtained a well-publicized divorce and her

children often were in the limelight. Even the president's mother, who was alive at the beginning of the New Deal, received some attention from the poets. They were all covered in one poem where Roosevelt was talking to Henry Ford.

> Says Franklin D., to Henry Ford,
> "I should be thankful to the Lord,
> My son, who is my friend and pal,
> I married off to that Du Pont gal.
>
> Another son I have made chief,
> He handles all the Bureaus' grief,
> When these come in from far and near,
> He'll never let them reach my ear.
>
> Then, there's my son in Harvard school,
> I tell you, Hank, the kid's no fool,
> He shot a cop with a B-B-gun,
> Then stood his ground and refused to run,
>
> For well he knew his illustrous dad,
> Would never think His son was bad,
> So, into Court, this son of mine
> Was taken, where he paid a fine.
>
> There's Sistie and Buzzie, and Anna, their mother,
> I swear you could not find another
> Family group in thhis broad land,
> With a record as good or achievements so grand.
>
> And there's Elinor, my own dear wife,
> Why, she's become a part of my daily life,
> As she roams the country, cutting capers,
> And head-lining all the daily papers.
>
> And my dear old mother, who's not yet gone,
> A grander matron never was born
> To mortals here upon this earth,—
> Of rugged character and sterling worth.[34]

A poet from Oklahoma got many of the family into his critical verses.

The King is in the White House
Handing out the money
The Queen is on the front page
Looking worse than funny
One Knave is up at Boston
Passing out the plums
While the Nation alphabetically
Is paying all the bums.

The Maid has gone to Reno
To can her marriage vows
Another Knave is in Texas
With the New Queen he espoused
The Nation feels discouraged
The "Blue Eagle" does not sing
Now isn't this a pretty dish
To set before the King.[35]

Eleanor Roosevelt was the lightning rod of the family. She was visible and she was vocal. She wrote a newspaper column called "My Day" and she often was heard on the radio. A poet previously quoted was tired of hearing her.

Then came Her Master's Voice
In a broadcasting car.
You could hear her everywhere -
Both near and far.
She told the women,
She told the men.
Sometimes by radio,
Sometimes by pen.[36]

A widely circulated poem critical of Roosevelt appeared under several names. In a long poem of complaints, it included one against the president's wife.

When I wanted to punish the folks you know,
I'd put my wife on the radio.[37]

One of the poems was a fictitious conversation between Roosevelt and Henry Ford. Ford was clearly bothered by the role the president's wife was playing.

As for me wife, she stays at home,
Has no desire away to roam
About the country---making speeches,
Kissing dirty-faced kids, or addressing preachers.

You'll never see her in the papers,
You'll never see her cutting capers
On mountain tops or on bathing beaches,
Or dressed in slacks or riding breeches.[38]

Another poem that was found in many places was called "Tired." One verse attacked Mrs. Roosevelt and the grandchildren. This verse did not appear in all versions of the poem, apparently because some people considered it in bad taste.

I'm tired seeing Eleanor on page one,
    Of each royal in-law and favorite son,
I'm tired of Sistie and Buzzie Dall,
    Nobody knows how I'm tired of it all.[39]

One of the poets added Roosevelt to the list and compared him to Caesar.

After this retinue, while the band played,
In a flag-draped car came the cause of the parade,
Waving to the crowd his high silk hat,
Forgetting all the promises that fell so flat,
Standing on the necks of his Favorable Press
He bore in his arms a radio address.
Roosevelt Second, the Voice with the brain,
With his family, fresh from the Reno train,
Rode to his triumph like a Caesar of old,
Throwing to the crowd the confiscated gold.[40]

For the opponents of Roosevelt who saw him as many of the poets did, their opportunity would be in 1936. Roosevelt clearly would run for reelection, but many of the opponents believed he had been shown for what he was and the voters would respond accordingly.

Some of the poets looked back to the pre-New Deal days when Republican prosperity seemed unlimited. Some of them longed for Hoover and hoped he would run again. One of the poets sent Hoover a poem that he hoped would help convince Hoover to run again.

There's a murmur growing louder
    Each day and every hour,
And like mighty giant powder
    Contains much hidden power.
The meaning of it is quite plain;
    Line up or clear the track,
And good times will return again,-
    Hoover's coming back.

For country's sake make no mistake,
    We've had enough - alack;
There is today no other way,
    Hoover must come back.

We need a fearless leader now,
    Who's able to command;
One who will stand upon the prow
    And there with steady hand
Direct the good old ship of state;
    Defend it from attack,-
We're calling him ere it's too late;
    Hoover's coming back.[41]

A man from Louisville, Kentucky, told Hoover what his reelection would mean.

If anything is left next year
Which I sometimes doubt and sometimes fear
God grant Mr. Hoover may come back
And Get us once more on the right Track.[42]

Even if Hoover were not the candidate, Republicans were the hope of most of Roosevelt's opponents. As a poet from Pittsburgh, Pennsylvania, said:

It is now late in 1935,
Still you want us to
Call you sweetheart
Old Democratic Party,
This longer we cannot do
For you failed to make good
The promises you made to
Your friends in 1932.

Dear Republican Party,
Let us call you sweetheart
For you are a lover true
And with New Deals and
Promises to my friends
We are through,
And we are sorry we were
So fickle in 1932,
In 1936 we will return to you.[43]

Another one told Hoover that his party had to come back to power to save the country from the same thing that happened to Russia.

Is it British? Is it Yiddish?
Who today can truly tell?
What a pity that the witty
Nevermore the Story quell.

Who is Master? Can he faster
Push the People into hell?
Now I wonder by the plunder
In few hands is said to dwell.

Is it Yiddish? Is it British
That is sapping Uncle Sam?
And the trouble! Bust the bubble
Of the Banks that build a dam?

Does he dare it? Will he share it
With the Russian Bolsheviks?
Not if Hearty Hoover Party
With the Golden Eagle shreiks.[44]

A poet from Los Angeles was afraid a Republican running under that label could not win.

The needful thing at present is a brand-new party name.
On which conservatives can all unite.
"Republicans" and "Democrats" are very much the same
And "Socialism," BOTH, desire to fight.[45]

Getting Southerners to vote for a Republican would probably be impossible, according to this poet. He had the answer and he concluded his poem with it.

> The patriotic members of this worthy ancient clan
> Would like to voice their protests forcefully.
> But find it hard to register and vote "Republican"
> E'en though, they with the pla tform, full agree.
>
> "A house that is divided" so 'tis said, must surely fall.
> Conservatives should rally to the cause.
> Agree upon a common name, acceptable to all-
> And jointly save the country's basic laws.[46]

Clearly, the enemy, these poets believed, was Roosevelt. He had to be stopped as far as they were concerned. One of the milder statements came from Long Island.

> For soon our ship will be sailing
>   Into Nineteen Thirty-Six.
> With the hopes that another election
>   Our country's ailments will fix.
>
> But our ship must have the right cargo
>   Aboard we must have the right crew,
> It must head in the right direction
>   And the man at the helm must be TRUE.[47]

A song writer sent a campaign song to Hoover in 1936 that portrayed Roosevelt as a dreamer.

> There's a dreamer in the White House,
> Building castles in the air,
> Like a child with lettered blocks,
> That he piles with greatest care.
> He named one castle N-R-A,
> Another I-E-C,
> With forty other lettered schemes,
> To bring prosperity.
>
> The squeals of butcher'd hogs foretold,
> The end of New Deal dreams,

For this White House dreamer's ways are bold,
Like all dictator's schemes,
Upon his alphabetic soup,
The country's fed up I'll say.
And he's getting us deeper in debt each day.

He's had his day.
Boondoggling's under ban.
In U.S.A.,
Dictators get the can.
So comes the end of New Deal dreams,
And all dictator's schemes.
In the President's chair he shall not stay.[48]

An unidentified poet became more personal in his attacks.

Election Day draws nearer,
When Franklin comes to scratch,
To stilt his Brand New Era,
He's sprung the Treas'ry latch !

YES : Frank's a Bunco Steerer !
NO : Ponzi's not his match !
SURE : Franklin's a High-Gearer,
To brood his speckled hatch !

The Treas'ry's close to busted,
But Frank dont give a Damn !
He'll blister with tax-mustard,
He's bled dry Uncle Sam !

The RICH he makes his target,
Like ev'ry Demagogue !
THE ISSUE - he will fog it !
Aint he a yaller Dog ![49]

A poet from Florida called Roosevelt every name he could think of.

The devil's in the saddle, as never known before;
He handles bit and bridle from shore to shore!
He thinks he's God Almighty, the ruler of all worlds;
He is a dictator, socialist, communist, he unfurls

His red flag in Washington, Chicago, and Philadelphia!
He commands, threatens, executes; it's "do as I say".
. . . . . . . . . . . . . . . . . . . . . . . . . .
America, America, the land of the free-born, awake!
You've lost your chart and compass, awake for Jesus sake!
Get busy, men of honor, we need some blood and thunder;
Taxes are alarming, deficits, and we wonder
What next -- but wait till nineteen thirty-six -
We'll expose their underhandedness and all their mean tricks.[50]

Another poet thought he ranked with the dictators of the world.

His pictures should hang in the galleries high
With Stalin's, Mussolini's, Hitler's, all that fry.
"Time rushes on!" Is his race run?
Has he finished the course or just begun?
Is he launching once more a great campaign
With his nefarious pledges to the voters again?
Will he be able to fool them with smiling gab?
Or will the voters decide he is screwy mad?[51]

One of the most controversial actions Roosevelt undertook had to do with the Supreme Court. Some historians believe it was his most serious political mistake, but others disagree. It is still an open question among historians.

During his first term Roosevelt had no opportunity to appoint members to the Supreme Court. All the justices were elderly or had been appointed by Republican presidents, except for those still on the Court appointed by the one Democratic president in recent memory, Woodrow Wilson. Most of them were conservative and proved to be antagonistic to most New Deal measures.

In May 1935 the Court invalidated the National Industrial Recovery Act (NIRA) which created the National Recovery Administration (NRA). It had been launched with much fanfare with the Blue Eagle as its symbol, but it had become a muddled mess. Some historians believe Roosevelt was not so upset by the Court's decision because it took him off the hook by eliminating a failed program. Even so, Roosevelt was outraged by the Court's reasoning and what he considered its thwarting of the public's wishes. When the Court invalidated the Agricultural Adjustment Act (AAA) in January 1936, Roosevelt and his supporters were truly outraged by what they considered capricious and arbitrary acts by nine men unresponsive to the public.

Some of the poets concurred in these opinions. A poet from Long Beach, California, was mild, but firm, in his attitudes about the Court.

> But the Big Boys are busy,
>     after every bill is passed
> Call it unconstitutional,
>     try to tie him hard and fast
> So if they can't get him,
>     through the mighty press
> They'll take it to the Supreme Court,
>     that's anyone's guess
> With all due respect,
>     to those nine good men
> Who can knock out a law,
>     with the stroke of a pen
> Because of the constitution,
>     that is one hundred fifty old
> Some laws need changing,
>     they do not fit I'm told
> If this is not correct,
>     why did we pass before
> Twenty one ammendments,
>     that proves there must be more
> Let Congress rule the country
>     and let the people say
> By use of the ballot,
>     the good old American way[52]

Others became more critical and personal about the members of the Court, as was the case of a poet from Jacksonville, Florida, in a long poem.

> You know this court is formed of nine grand-fathers
> Nine aged men all wedded to the past.
> Nine victims of senility's weak sorrows,
> Who cannot see a worth-while change would last.
> You know this court of nine was not elected,
> But just appointed by some whim or will,
> Of those whom we have since repudiated,
> But now these nine must linger with us still.

They hold themselves above our people's voting,
They count themselves beyond our congress too.
A life-time job themselves they are promoting,
Regardless of our rights, or justice true.
They take unto themselves to block our progress,
These nine who say us nay when e'er they choose.
They make a JOKE of Government of the People,
Our GAINS, they CLAIM the right to make us LOSE.[53]

The same poet followed up a few weeks later with another that was more critical. The poet was clearly concerned about the Court.

They know supreme court rulings by nine appointed men,
Are hostile to all humane laws, and will be to the end.
They know interpretation as far as theyre concerned--
Are just opinions of these nine -- things personally spurned.
The Court should be impartial, in constitution's rules,
But they twist it to suit their views and take us all for fools.
Now these who haven't brains or guts, to changes bring about,
Will find at next election time, they all will be kicked out.

The Constitution does not say a Judge can rule by whim,
Nor have the hellish power to balk, all laws displeasing him.
The Constitution specifys the power all shall hold,-
And no-where does it preference give to those who worship gold.
For the General Welfare Congress has the power to provide,
The Judges do Impeachment rate when this they over-ride.
Precisely and IMPARTIALLY they are SUPPOSED to stand,
Interpreting REGARDLESS of THEIR views on EITHER hand.[54]

Some were frustrated because they saw the Court as arbitrarily interfering in the humane efforts of Roosevelt to help the nation. A poet from New Jersey reflected this.

When the world is topsy-turvy and your Uncle Sam-u-el
    Tries to bring our nation back to prosperous times--
Giving starving millions food and idle hands some work,
    Seeking thus to lessen social crimes--
He is halted in his action and his efforts put to naught
    By nine aged men with robes that do appal:
They declare it can't be done--the reason would you know?
    Because it is UN-CON-STI-TU-TION-AL![55]

A poet from Chicago believed the Court was overstepping its legal authority.

> There is no act, there is no word,
> Within our constitution,
> To give the power to a few,
> To overrule the nation.
>
> The peoples mandate is supreme
> No court can 'er discard it,
> Nor question rights of free born men,
> Their duty is to guard it;
>
> And when they fail their sacred trust,
> Unworthy of their vestment,
> The judges then must stand at trail,
> And ours shall be the judgement.[56]

Some poets were optimistic that Roosevelt would prevail over this obstacle. A poet from Corona, New York, was confident.

> Recovery, his pet ambition, thrives,
> In spite of those who try success to block.
> Although they hamper, criticise and knock,
> Nine Men 'ganged up' cant stop his helpful drives.[57]

A poet from Ohio sent three poems, two of which concerned the Court and encouraged Roosevelt.

> A DECISION OF ANY COURT SUPREME
> CANNOT DO AWAY WITH RIGHT:
> FOR RIGHT IS, AND FOREVERMORE WILL BE
> FAR SUPERIOR TO MIGHT:
> FOUNDED ON TRUTH AND JUSTICE THERE IT STANDS,
> AGAINST IT NAUGHT WILL E'ER PREVAIL,
> ON IT ARE BASED ALL OF OUR GOD'S COMMANDS:
> US IN DISTRESS 'TWILL NEVER FAIL.[58]

The poets were only a small segment of those bothered by the actions of the Court. Shortly after winning reelection in 1936, Roosevelt unveiled a plan in February 1937 to enlarge the Court. His goal was to add members who would be favorable to New Deal measures. It was a transparent effort to get his measures supported and it caused a storm of protest, among both Republicans and Democrats. Some people who had been strong New Deal supporters broke with Roosevelt over this matter, never to return. Many of them saw it as a dictatorial power-grab that violated the spirit, if not the letter, of the Constitution.

Four people sent a poem to James Farley in March 1937 stating their objections to the Court change. They signed the poem, "From Four of Your Best Friends."

> In Lincolns day the Supreme Court
>     Now showa DECAY T'was but a DREAM -
> And so I bid you High and Low,
>     To let this Court These OLD MEN GO,
> Our President is full of words,
>     Most TREASONABLE that Peoples HEARD
> He WOULD upset WITH HIS NEW DEAL
>     A Country built on woe and weal;
> I'm Just a LITTLEFELLOW . . . ME!!
>     But I say NO and so SHOULD THEE,
> THE PRESIDENT would be Supreme,
>     'Tis power HE wants it is HIS DREAM
> This Court he HATES, now CUTS HIS DEAL -
>     He'd LIKE to grind them neath his heel.[59]

One of the widely circulated poems called "Rejected" and sometimes "You Can't Stay Here" fantasized about Roosevelt standing at the gates of Hell. He had to tell the Devil of all the bad things he had done so he could get in. In a long litany were a few lines about his actions regarding the Court.

> When they got too strong on certain things
> I'd pack and head for old Warm Springs
> I ruined their country, their homes, and then
> I placed the blame on nine old men."[60]

Another of the poems passed from hand to hand was "Traitors Three," which concerned a conversation among Brutus, Benedict Arnold, and Roosevelt in which each one talked about the terrible things they had done. Regarding the Court, Roosevelt said:

> I fooled those YOKELS, both old and young,
> I was the greatest scoundrel to remain unhung.

I ruined the country, MY FRIENDS, and then
I placed the blame on "NINE OLD MEN."[61]

One poet praised the Court for killing—or trying to kill—the Blue Eagle and preventing Roosevelt from becoming a Mussolini.

Let's stand for the Constitution
It's good enough for me.
I'll change for no dictatorship,
As in MUSOLITALY
Our nine good men brought the eagle low;
They took away beak and claw,
It's squawk is with us still, but weak,
For they also broke it's jaw.[62]

Another poet thought the Court was doing the right thing and that Roosevelt might be mad.

Head on into the Supreme Court he smashed,
It's the one last gate to be crashed,
When he thought all was in the bag,
He ran into the Constitutional snag.
Watching our liberties as a Court to judge,
As between good laws and sweetened fudge,
This wise old Court gave its decision
Throwing the Blue Bird's twitters into derision.
His Birdie was cooked. It hurt so bad, -
He couldn't take it. Is he mad?[63]

Roosevelt lost the battle to enlarge the Court. Congress was unable to pass legislation that would allow it. The Court recognized, however, the direction of the political winds and began to modify some of its decisions. Finally, some members began to retire, giving Roosevelt a chance to make his own appointments. Eventually, most of the major New Deal legislation survived legal challenges. Some historians concluded that Roosevelt lost the battle but won the war.

By 1939 some people were still discussing the Court fight. One poet took the opportunity to revise the poem "Rejected" to make it favorable to Roosevelt. Clearly, he supported Roosevelt's position on the Court.

You prompted my critics to raise up a snort
When I wanted new blood in 'Old Whiskers' Court

For those 'Nine Old Fossils' living back in the day;
Of the long-legged boot and the old one-horse shay.[64]

Other than the Court fight, the most controversial decision of Roosevelt was to run for a third term in 1940. This was such a break with tradition that Roosevelt lost many of his Democratic supporters. Even his vice president, John Nance Garner, broke with Roosevelt because he believed it was now his turn to be president.

By the time of the election of 1940 the number of poems sent to Roosevelt and Hoover had declined, probably because of increased prosperity and more interest in the war which began in Europe in 1939. Even so, a few poets responded to the third term issue. A woman from North Carolina welcomed the idea of Roosevelt's serving a third term.

The Father of our Country,a precedent, did set
Revolutionary ideas, now are passe,you bet.
Though we are still Jefferson Democrats
We're a peoples union,not plutocrats,not autocrats.

We want Mr.Roosevelt for the third term
It makes no difference how REPUBLICANS and ANTIS squirm.
He is the only man for President to whom we should bow ?
Whom I know, can mostly have his way and without a row .

Just think of our Land of the FREE & the BRAVE,
To be dominated by a Hoover,a Hitler or some other Zouave.
Oh, Democracy & Roosevelt both,thou art a jewel,
Of your able understanding,we want a third term renewal.
. . . . . . . . . . . . . . . . . . . . . . . . . . . . . . .
North Carolina people and the South,both great & small,
Regardless of Bailey,our Bob,but all
Will welcome you back in the Presidential Saddle,
And the issue we'll most certainly not straddle .

None but TEXANS want Cactus Jack,
Inability. Yet alert in cards to stack.
So why decline ? Statesmen are so few
We want a mighty man and that is U-U-U .[65]

A woman from Missouri was complimentary of Roosevelt and said he had been a good president. But he should not violate tradition.

Come sit close by, Franklin D.,
   And let's, you and I, have a chat
About this "THIRD TERM" they're talking about
   Also the "NEW DEAL" and this and that.

I think that most all the people, Frank,
   Think that you're a mighty fine fellow,
But, when the talk is of a "THIRD TERM"
   That's more than they care to swallow.

I think that the way you took care of us
   When work, men, could not find,
Proved, to us, that you have a heart
   You are so considerate and kind.

The men have jobs and are working, now,
   Their families to clothe and feed,
But listen, Frank, when it comes to a "THIRD TERM"
   Will be one time they will not heed.

But, Frank, you're too much of a man, to ask
   For a "THIRD TERM," to be elected again,
For, you know, that from our "FOREFATHERS" on down
   A "THIRD TERM" is considered a-----"SIN."

So, Frank, I know as sure as I'm sitting here,
   That you hold the welfare of your people too dear
To ask for a "THIRD TERM," or anything else
   That would not leave your conscience-----"CLEAR."[66]

The criticism of Roosevelt, his family, and the people in his admin-
istration took many forms. Stories and jokes—some in bad taste—
circulate about all presidents, and Roosevelt was no exception. Some of
these poems have been mentioned already. One was called "Traitors
Three" in which Brutus, Benedict Arnold, and Roosevelt try to top each
other about how bad they were in their lifetimes. The poem ends with
the following verse:

Brutus stood there filled with awe,
Arnold sat with fallen jaw,
The Brutus said "We've had our fling,
Get up now, Arnold, and salute your KING."[67]

In a similar vein was the poem called "Rejected," but occasionally titled "You Can't Stay Here." In this poem Roosevelt stands before the gates of Hell seeking to get in. Roosevelt cites his many crimes and evil acts against the American people to justify his place in Hell. At the end the Devil responds:

> And the Devil stood and his head he bowed.
> "At last," he said, "let's make it clear,
> You'll have to move; you can't stay here!
> For once you mingle with this mob,
> I'll have to hunt myself another job."[68]

Occasionally, Roosevelt supporters rewrote these poems to put Roosevelt in a good light by reciting his many accomplishments.[69]

Another poem that was widely circulated was called "Tired." It was a recitation of many of Roosevelt's actions and ended with a plea.

> I'm tired and bored with the whole New Deal
> With its juggler's smile, its barker's spiel
> Dear Lord, out of thy available men
> Please grant us a Cleveland or Coolidge again.[70]

As was true of Hoover and presidents since, Roosevelt was the subject of rewritten versions of the 23rd Psalm. Most of them were not very original and criticized him for unemployment, depression, high taxes, and various other problems.[71] One of them was a bit more imaginative.

> Thou art "my friend." I shall not worry.
> Thou makest me to rest upon the shovel; thou
> leadest me along the pleasant paths of life.
> Thou lightenest my burdens and teachest me the
> way of easy money for thine own glory.
> Yea, though I walk through a slight recession, I
> will fear no labor; for thou wilt keep me; thy Bureaus
> and Administrations will look after me.
> Thou preparest a pension for me in the days of
> my youth; thou fillest my life with leisure; my mind
> is at rest.
> Surely *someone* will foot the bills and I will
> abide in peace and plenty forever.[72]

One of the poets rewrote the Lord's Prayer to be critical of Roosevelt. It was titled "Prayer of the—New Deal 1938."

> Our President, who art in Washington,
> Great should be thy shame;
> If thou keepest on, it will be done as it is in Germany;
> Give us this day untaxed bread and
>     Forgive us our tax evasions
> As ye forgave J. P. Morgan;
> And lead us not to Communism;
> Deliver us from Dictatorship,
>     For such is the Power and the Glory of the Democrats.[73]

Roosevelt certainly generated strong emotions—for and against him. His appeal and the hatred expressed toward him have never been fully understood. Whatever the answer may be, the impact of Roosevelt on the country was as great as any president. A woman expressed the hatred as clearly as anyone could.

> We HATE roosevelt!
> We HATE roosevelt!
> We HATE roosevelt !
> May he burn eternally in hell.[74]

This poet went ahead to include a letter that expressed as much venom as anyone had.

> Will we co-operate? Booooooooooo! He has asked for hate. Now he is going to get it. He has turned American against American. We intend to stay turned. There is more bitterness and hatred in America today than there was even during the Civil War, because at that time there was a man in the White House who could at least make some people love him. NOT ONE VOTER has any love for roosevelt. All the love in the campaign went to the man whose shoe roosevelt is not fit to touch. That man could have united America. That man could have helped England and thus helped the world. Roosevelt breeds only hate and if he had to depend on his own efforts he would have starved to death long ago, so incompetent is he. Booooooooooo! Booooooooooo to roosevelt the incompetent man. Booooooo to roosevelt the Hitler of America! We HATE roosevelt. We will hate him as long as there is breath in our body. We will work against him as long as there is breath in

our body. We HATE roosevelt. He has turned America into a madhouse of HATE. Booooooooooo![75]

Another poet who included a number of critical poems in his letter wrote one in Italian dialect.

> Last veek, I hear two feller talk on da San'
> 'Bout feller called "Frankie", big President man,
> I don't hear so good wot day say in da speech,
> But it soun' like he too is a Sonna da Beach.
>
> Now I don' teenk dey mean he be feller like me,
> 'Cause he don' leeve here, on a da Beach by da Sea
> So I don't onnerstand; maybe him an' me each,
> Be two deeferen' kind of a Sonna da Beach.
>
> Vell, I'm joost "Tony" da Dago, an' dam glad I am
> I'm glad I ain't, wot you call, President Man,
> 'Cause some day, ven I die an' "Heaven" I reach,
> Dey will say "HI Tony; Come in, You Sonna da Beach".[76]

A poet from Long Island thought Roosevelt was cynical and uncaring.

> To be Supreme I have aspired.
> Unlimited powers I've acquired.
> Good man and true I have had fired.
> But ---
>     I'm going on a cruise.
>
> I know full well the country's debt
> Is caused by me; but I should fret.
> I feel entangled in a net.
> So ---
>     I'm going on a cruise.
>
> I see my country going to hell
> Handwriting on the wall doth spell
> Destruction. But --- Oh well!
>     I'm going on a cruise.
>
> Just what new plan I'll hatch up next
> Or where you'll find my next scheme's text

I cannot say; I am perplexed.
So ---
    I'm going on a cruise.[77]


A poem titled "What Roosevelt Should Do" and published in an unidentified newspaper seemed to sum up most of the criticism of Roosevelt.

Started NEW DEAL agitation.
Staged a marv'lous preparation
For the downfall of the nation.
With his drum and fife.

But the NEW DEAL incantation
Drew Supreme Court's condemnation
Consequent humiliation
'Mid the growing strife.

Brought upon us tribulation
Sponsoring lawless legislation
Taxes without limitation
Cutting us like a knife.

Who, in all the whole creation
Ever wrought such consternation
To the heart of this great nation
With disturbance rife.

Now we'll make this peroration;
Franklin's filled us with vexation,
He should take a long vacation
Lasting all his life.[78]


Without doubt, those who disliked Roosevelt were not shy about their feelings. Even though they were vocal, they clearly were in the minority, as witnessed by Roosevelt's continued winning election after election. The volume of critical poetry was also much smaller than those favorable to him.

# 9

# Conclusion

Poetry clearly was an important form of communication with Presidents Hoover and Roosevelt during the Great Depression. The poets who labored over their work and took the time to compose lines were interested in the world around them. That they would produce these labors of love or verses of complaint speaks clearly to their belief that change could come and that it would be for the better.

The poets of the 1930s did not write about everything that happened. They concentrated on events, programs, or people they knew and understood and were willing to send their opinions with the hope that their voices would be heard. Citizens have always communicated with their leaders to influence public affairs. The most common forms of communication were letters and telegrams. Sometimes their attempts to influence public officials were brief, succinct letters that made a point without taking the time of busy persons. There were some, of course, who wrote extensive letters and even enclosed detailed plans of what they wanted done. Some of the letter-writers wrote regularly and often to presidents and other leaders, particularly those they thought would listen to them and possibly follow their advice.

For them to take the time to put their thoughts in verse form might not be expected on first glance. Yet, when one understands that poetry had always been a part of American reading habits before World War II, it seems only reasonable that citizens would use this technique to tell their leaders what they thought.

Undoubtedly, some of the amateur poets had ulterior motives for sending their verses to the presidents. Some wanted fame and others wanted to have the power of influencing public policy. Some wanted to make money from their work. They believed that their work was good and that they needed only someone with influence who could make their poems or songs famous. If they could get their poems set to music and played on the radio, they would get rich. Considering how much many people were suffering from the hard times of the 1930s, a little fame or a little money would have meant much to them.

Despite their motives, the poets do reflect public sentiment during the depression. Their work tends to follow the general pattern of public opinion as has been shown through various studies of the period. They reflected the hope, the optimism, the suffering, and the despair of the times. The way they expressed their opinions indicate the degree of suffering or the intensity of their feelings about certain leaders or programs of the government.

Even though surveys of the other libraries of presidents since Roosevelt do not reveal the amount of poetry that exists in either the Hoover or the Roosevelt libraries, one cannot assume that the writing of poetry to public officials suddenly ended in 1945. As already noted, public acceptance and the popularity of poetry declined in the post-war years, but certainly people continued to write verse. Apparently, they did not send their work to presidents as they did in the 1930s.

The other presidential libraries may have poetry written by average citizens, but they are not organized in such a way as to make it readily available. At the time later presidents were in office, those persons who handled the mail may not have realized that original poetry was arriving on a regular basis and in handling the mail, they did not separate it or make notations of it. When the presidential libraries were organized, the archivists were first concerned about cataloging the documents and papers relating to major events. Constituent mail probably was placed in a fairly low priority. In fact, some of the constituent mail may well have never been sorted, cataloged, or organized as it has been in the Hoover and Roosevelt libraries.

Letter writing continues today and the volume of mail for each president continues to increase. Later presidential staffs may not have kept all correspondence as was done earlier. It is possible that samples were kept and tallies were kept for the presidents about the trends that appeared in the mail received. Communication from average persons is a difficult primary source to use and evaluate, but it can be enlightening, as the work of the poets in the 1930s reveals.

Future historians will have even more difficulty in analyzing the opinions of letter writers because of changing technology. President Bill Clinton has begun a new practice by installing an electronic mail system that allows people to send messages instantaneously through the computer on the technology called the Internet. Early reports indicate that the volume of mail coming into the White House over this system is very large.

Whether the electronic mail is being saved and archived is not known. If it is not being kept, that will be a major loss to future historians. At the present time, there is no way to know exactly what kinds of mail President Clinton is receiving, but one can easily speculate about it. One question about it that pertains to this study is whether today's users of modern technology are sending their opinions to the president in verse form—and if they are, how extensive it is. If people are still sending the opinions in verse form, it will reveal how they feel about things that are happening in the 1990s just as the poets did in the 1930s.

The poems of the depression reveal public sentiment at the time. The poetry shows how serious the economic depression was and how people reacted to it. It indicates a sense of hope and optimism that one probably would not find in similar material today. The depression poets believed that improvement could come and the majority of them were willing to use the government to bring change. One could easily assume that today's poetry—if it exists—might well reflect opposite opinions about the public's attitude toward government.

Certainly, the depression poets were a cross-section of the public at large. Their views were similar to the opinions of the general public, as other studies reveal. Social and economic conditions of the 1930s can be seen in the poetry. There is much room for further research in this material.

The poets were average persons who had a way of expressing themselves through verse. Some of the poetry may not have been very good as poetry, but it was excellent as a reflection of the society in which the poet lived. History is really the story of people and the times in which they lived. Nothing gives a better understanding of the way people lived—their fears, frustrations, suffering, and successes—than the poetry that came from the heart. Much or most of these poems were never read by more than a handful of people. They are truly a glimpse into the minds of the people.

This poetry is a major source of the social history of twentieth-century America. Perhaps this study will reveal some of the value to be gained from this type of research and others will use the material for other historical and scholarly studies.

# Notes

## Chapter 1

1. Quoted in John F. Kennedy, *Profiles in Courage* (New York: Harper, 1955), 10.

2. Democratic National Committee (DNC) Collection, Franklin D. Roosevelt Library, Hyde Park, N.Y., December 24, 1932, Box 736. Hereafter cited as DNC, FDRL.

3. *Ibid.*

4. McCowen to Roosevelt, December 31, 1932, FDRL.

5. Secretary to Mr. Roosevelt to McCowen, February 18, 1933, FDRL.

6. A thorough study of the letters written to President Franklin Roosevelt is Leila A. Sussmann, *Dear FDR: A Study of Political Letter Writing* (Totowa, N.J.: Bedminster Press, 1963).

7. Ira Smith, *Dear Mr. President* (New York: Julian Mesner, 1949).

8. Sussmann, *Dear FDR.*

9. George Wolfskill and John A. Hudson, *All But the People: Franklin D. Roosevelt and His Critics, 1933-39* (New York: Macmillan, 1969).

10. *Ibid.*, 345.

11. Robert S. McElvaine, *Down and Out in the Great Depression: Letters from the Forgotten Man* (Chapel Hill: University of North Carolina Press, 1983).

12. Gerald Markowitz and David Rosner, eds., *"Slaves of the Depression": Workers' Letters About Life on the Job* (Ithaca, N.Y., Cornell University Press, 1987).

13. Sussman, *Dear FDR*, 3-4.

14. Lucas Carpenter, "Academic Poetry That Has No Place in the Real World," *Chronicle of Higher Education*, August 3, 1994, A44.

15. For a discussion of how government officials attempted to build confidence and the denial of a depression, see Donald W. Whisenhunt, *The Depression in Texas: The Hoover Years* (New York: Garland, 1983).

## Chapter 2

1. Many excellent studies are available on Herbert Hoover and his career. See, for example, Joan Hoff-Wilson, *Herbert Hoover, Forgotten Progressive*

(Boston: Little, Brown, 1975); Gene Smith, The Shattered Dream: Herbert Hoover and the Great Depression (New York: McGraw Hill, 1984); David Burner, Herbert Hoover: A Public Life (New York: Knopf, 1979); Martin L. Fausold, The Presidency of *Herbert Hoover* (Lawrence: University Press of Kansas, 1985).

2. N.d., Herbert Hoover Presidential Library, Presidential Papers Subject —Poems, Box 92. Hereafter cited as HHPL. No identification of the authors of the poems and songs will be made. Citations will be to the location of the material.

3. N.d., HHPL, Presidential Personal—Poets, Poetry, Box 85.

4. January 18, 1931, HHPL, Poetry 1931, Box 222.

5. October 5, 1928, *Ibid.*, Songs (1), Box 95.

6. N.d., *Ibid.*, Songs, Box 95.

7. N.d., *Ibid.*, Poems, Box 92.

8. N.d., *Ibid.*, Songs (1), Box 95.

9. N.d., *Ibid.*, Poetry sent to HH 1933-64 (1), Box 135.

10. N.d., *Ibid.*, Poems, Box 92.

11. N.d., *Ibid.*, Songs, Box 95.

12. N.d., Songs (1), Box 95.

13. *Ibid.*

14. *Ibid.*

15. N.d., *Ibid.*, Box 92.

16. *Ibid.*

17. *Ibid.*

18. N.d. *Ibid.*, Poems, Box 95. Similar poems of this sort may be found in Box 95.

19. *Ibid.*, Songs (1), Box 95.

20. N.d., *Ibid.*, Poems, Box 92.

21. *Ibid.*

22. October 16, 1930, *Ibid.*, Poetry 1929-1930, Box 222.

23. May 13, 1932, *Ibid.*, Poetry 1932, Box 223.

24. N.d., *Ibid*, Box 223.

25. August 23, 1932, *Ibid.*, Poetry 1932, August, Box 223.

26. N.d., *Ibid*, Poetry 1933 & undated, Box 224.

27. *Ibid.*

28. October 13, 1930, *Ibid.*, Poetry 1929-1930, Box 222.

29. *Ibid.*

30. March 27, 1932, *Ibid.*, Poetry 1932, January-March, Box 222.

31. August 3, 1932, *Ibid.*, Poetry 1932, August, Box 223.

32. N.d., *Ibid*, Poetry 1932, September 1-15, Box 223.

33. October 6, 1932, *Ibid.*, Poetry 1932, October 6-10, Box 224.

34. *Ibid.*

35. January 22, 1932, *Ibid.*, Poetry 1932, January-March, Box 222.

36. October 6, 1932, *Ibid.*, Poetry 1932, October 6-10, Box 224.

37. May 25, 1932, *Ibid.*, Poetry 1932, May, Box 223.

38. October 25, 1932, *Ibid.*, Poetry 1932, October 25, Box 224.

39. August 23, 1932, *Ibid.*, Poetry 1932, August, Box 223.

40. July 8, 1932, *Ibid.*, Poetry 1932, June-July, Box 223.

41. February 19, 1932, *Ibid.*, Poetry 1932, January-March, Box 222.

42. September 1, 1931, *Ibid.*, Poetry 1931, Box 222.

43. June 4, 1931, *Ibid.*

44. September 26, 1932, *Ibid.*, Poetry 1932, September 26, Box 223.

45. N.d., *Ibid.*, Poetry 1932, October 1-5, Box 223.

46. October 9, 1931, *Ibid.*, Poetry 1931, Box 222.

47. November 2, 1932, *Ibid.*, Poetry 1932, November 1-5, Box 224.

48. April 17, 1932, *Ibid.*, Poetry 1932, April, Box 223.

49. September 15, 1930, *Ibid.*, Poetry 1929-1930, Box 222.

50. N.d., *Ibid.*, Poetry 1932, November 6-15, Box 224.

51. September 29, 1932, *Ibid.*, Poetry 1932, September 29, Box 223.

52. March 5, 1932, *Ibid.*, Poetry 1932, January-March, Box 222.

53. August 18, 1932, *Ibid.*, Poetry 1932, August, Box 223.

54. August 22, 1931, *Ibid.*, Poetry 1931, Box 222.

55. N.d., *Ibid.*, Poetry 1932, January-March, Box 222.

56. July 24, 1931, *Ibid.*, Poetry 1931, Box 222.

57. *Ibid.*

58. November 9, 1932, *Ibid.*, Poetry 1932, November 16-30, Box 224.

59. February 1, 1933, *Ibid.*, Poetry 1933 & undated, Box 224.

60. *Ibid.*

61. February 5, 1993, *Ibid.*

62. November 9, 1932, *Ibid.*, Poetry 1932, November 16-30, Box 224.

63. January 4, 1933, *Ibid.*, Poetry 1933, & undated, Box 224.

64. October 28, 1938, *Ibid.*, Poetry sent to HH 1933-64 (2), Box 135.

65. N.d., *Ibid.*

66. *Ibid.*

67. N.d., *Ibid.*

68. N.d., *Ibid.*

69. N.d., *Ibid.*

70. August 10, 1954, *Ibid.*

*Chapter 3*

1. Franklin D. Roosevelt Library (FDRL), September 17, 1935, Official File (OF), Box 6.

2. *Ibid.*, January 29, 1936, Box 9.

3. *Ibid.*

4. HHPL, Presidential Papers—Subject—Poetry, May 9, 1932, Box 223.

5. FDRL, June 27, 1934, OF616, Box 3.

6. *Ibid.*

7. *Ibid.*, October 18, 1935, Box 6.

8. HHPL, Presidential Papers—Subject—Poetry, September 30, 1932, Box 223.

9. *Ibid.*

10. *Ibid.*

11. *Ibid.*

12. FDRL, Democratic National Committee (DNC) Files, November 3, 1932, Box 732.

13. HHPL, Presidential Papers—Subject—Poetry, April 26, 1932, Box 223.

14. FDRL, n.d., OF616, Box 1.

15. *Ibid.*, n.d., Box 10.

16. *Ibid.*

17. Quoted by Theodore Saloutos and John D. Hicks, *Agricultural Discontent in the Middle West, 1900-1939* (Madison: University of Wisconsin Press, 1951).

18. FDRL, n.d., OF616, Box 9.

19. *Ibid.*, June 27, 1934, Box 3.

20. *Ibid.*, November 1, 1934.

21. *Ibid.*, April 15, 1936, Box 10.

22. For an analysis of the cotton moratorium controversy see Donald W. Whisenhunt, "Huey Long and the Texas Cotton Acreage Control Law of 1931," *Louisiana Studies*, 13 (1974).

23. FDRL, 1935, OF616, Box 9.

24. *Ibid.*, December 6, 1936, OF104, 1933-36 B.

25. *Ibid.*

26. For a discussion of the transient issue in Texas, see Donald W. Whisenhunt, "The Transient in the Depression," *Red River Valley Historical Review*, 1 (Spring, 1974).

27. FDRL, January 15, 1936, OF616, Box 9.

28. *Ibid.*, July 30, 1939, OF104, 1937-39 A-C.

29. *Ibid.*, November 11, 1934, OF616, Box 3.

30. *Ibid.*

31. *Ibid.*, n.d., OF104, 1933-36 B.

32. *Ibid.*, February 23, 1933, OF104, Box 1.

33. *Ibid.*, November 3, 1934, OF616, Box 3.

34. *Ibid.*, October 16, 1936, Box 11.

35. Thomas Minehan, *Boy and Girl Tramps of America* (New York: Farrar and Rinehart, 1934). Reprint in Americana Library Edition with introduction by Donald W. Whisenhunt (Seattle: University of Washington Press, 1976).

36. FDRL, October 18, 1935, OF616, Box 6.

37. *Ibid.*, December 31, 1934, Box 4.

38. *Ibid.*, October 18, 1935, Box 6.

39. *Ibid.*, November 1, 1934, Box 3.

40. *Ibid.*, February 23, 1933, OF104, Box 1.

41. For the reaction of one state, see Donald W. Whisenhunt, *The Depression in Texas: The Hoover Years* (New York: Garland, 1983).

## Chapter 4

1. David A. Shannon, *Between the Wars: America, 1919-1941* (Boston: Houghton Mifflin, 1965), 122-123.

2. "Letters From Readers," *Dallas Morning News*, January 14, 1931.

3. December 26, 1939, FDRL, OF616, Box 15.

4. November 4, 1932, HHPL, Poetry 1932, November 1-5, Box 224.

5. November 2, 1932, *Ibid.*

6. March 25, 1932, HHPL, Poetry 1932, January-March, Box 222.

7. August 20, 1932, HHPL, Poetry 1932, August, Box 223.

8. October 18, 1935, FDRL, OF616, Box 6.

9. April 24, 1932, HHPL, Poetry 1932, April, Box 223.

10. Cyclone Davis, *Memoirs* (Sherman, Texas: Courier Press, 1935), 98.

11. October 5, 1932, FDRL, DNC, Box 319.

12. March 9, 1938, FDRL, OF616, Box 14.

13. March 29, 1939, FDRL, OF616, Box 15.

14. January 15, 1936, FDRL, OF616, Box 9.

15. N.d., HHPL, Poetry 1932, September 1-15, Box 223.

16. December 25, 1939, FDRL, OF104, 1939 N-Z.

17. November 6, 1936, FDRL, OF616, Box 11.

18. Davis, *Memoir*, 45.

19. N.d., FDRL, OF616, Box 6.

20. January 25, 1937, OF104 1939 N-Z.

21. November 20, 1932, FDRL, DNC, Box 322.

22. October 8, 1932, FDRL, DNC, Box 308.

23. July 13, 1932, HHPL, Poetry 1932, June-July, Box 223.

24. March 9, 1938, FDRL, OF616, Box 14.

25. N.d., FDRL, OF616, Box 13.

26. October 24, 1932, FDRL, DNC, Box 568.

27. April 11, 1932, FDRL, DNC, Box 369.

28. March 29, 1932, FDRL, DNC, Box 720.

29. June 31 [*sic*], 1934, FDRL, OF616, Box 3.

30. June 29, 1936, FDRL, OF616, Box 10.

31. December 6, 1936, FDRL, OF104, 1933-36B.

32. October 4, 1936, FDRL, OF104, 1933-36B.

33. N.d., FDRL, OF616, Box 3.

34. August 6, 1932, FDRL, DNC, Box 16.

35. October 21, 1932, FDRL, DNC, Box 148.

36. July 6, 1932, FDRL, DNC, Box 724.

37. August 18, 1932, FDRL, DNC, Box 728.

38. November 18, 1932, FDRL, DNC, Box 736.

39. October 23, 1932, FDRL, DNC, Box 727.

40. N.d., FDRL, DNC, Box 718.

41. N.d., FDRL, OF616, Box 10.

42. August 1, 1935, FDRL, OF616, Box 6.

43. January 9, 1936, FDRL, OF616, Box 9.

44. N.d., FDRL, OF616, Box 9.

45. N.d., HHPL, Songs, Box 95.

46. N.d., HHPL, Songs, Box 95.

47. July 27, 1932, FDRL, DNC, Box 308.

48. January 15, 1932, HHPL, Poetry 1933 & undated, Box 224.

49. N.d., HHPL, Poetry sent to H.H. 1933-64 (2), Box 135.


*Chapter 5*


1. September 23, 1932, FDRL, DNC, Box 16.

2. April 11, 1932, *Ibid.*, Box 232.

3. October 31, 1932, *Ibid.*, Box 233.

4. November 1, 1932, *Ibid.*, Box 16.

5. December 1, 1933, FDRL, OF616, Box 1.

6. March 4, 1933, *Ibid.*

7. *Ibid.*

8. October 27, 1933, FDRL, OF616, Box 1.

9. April 8, 1933, FDRL, OF104 1933-36 N-P.

10. March 30, 1933, FDRL, OF104, Box 1.

11. N.d., FDRL, OF616, Box 1.

12. May 6, 1933, *Ibid.*

13. December 6, 1933, FDRL, OF104 1933-36 H-J.

14. August 15, 1934, *Ibid.*

15. 1934, FDRL, OF616, Box 2.

16. May 15, 1937, FDRL, OF41, Box 28.

17. January 22, 1935, FDRL, OF616, Box 4.
18. November 6, 1936, FDRL, OF616, Box 11.
19. N.d., FDRL, DNC, Box 735.
20. N.d., FDRL, OF616, Box 10.
21. March 13, 1939, FDRL, OF104 1937-39 I-M.
22. January 10, 1934, FDRL, OF104 1933-36 C.
23. June 22, 1936, FDRL, OF616, Box 10.
24. June 20, 1936, *Ibid.*
25. August 13, 1936, *Ibid.*, Box 11.
26. July 2, 1936, *Ibid.*, Box 10.
27. August 16, 1937, *Ibid.*, Box 13.
28. N.d., *Ibid.*, Box 6.
29. August 2, 1935, *Ibid.*
30. June 11, 1935, *Ibid.*, Box 5.
31. January 11, 1934, *Ibid.*, Box 2.
32. June 27, 1939, *Ibid.*, Box 3.
33. January 8, 1935, *Ibid.*, Box 4.
34. N.d., *Ibid.*, Box 9.
35. January 15, 1937, *Ibid.*, Box 12.
36. 1935, *Ibid.*, Box 8.
37. August 10, 1935, *Ibid.*, Box 6.
38. October 29, 1936, FDRL, OF104 1933-36 C.
39. July 7, 1936, FDRL, OF104, Box 1.
40. April 15, 1936, FDRL, OF616, Box 10.
41. January 15, 1936, *Ibid.*, Box 9.
42. September 11, 1936, OF104 1933-36 C.
43. *Ibid.*
44. October 17, 1936, FDRL, OF104 1933-36 B.
45. September 27, 1937, FDRL, OF616, Box 14.
46. October 16, 1939, FDRL, OF104 1937-39 I-M.
47. November 21, 1939, FDRL, OF616, Box 15.

*Chapter 6*

1. N.d., FDRL, OF616, Box 1.
2. August 26, 1933, FDRL, OF104, Box 1.
3. August 21, 1933, *Ibid.*
4. November 11, 1933, *Ibid.*
5. September 24, 1933, FDRL, OF616, Box 1.
6. September 14, 1933, *Ibid.*
7. November 17, 1933, FDRL, OF104, Box 1.

8. August 5, 1933, FDRL, OF104 1933-36 N-P.

9. September 6, 1933, FDRL, OF104 1933-36 H-J.

10. March 9, 1934, FDRL, OF104, Box 1.

11. August 4, 1940, FDRL, OF104, Box 4.

12. May 30, 1935, FDRL, OF616, Box 6.

13. January 15, 1936, FDRL, OF616, Box 9.

14. October 25, 1933, FDRL, OF616, Box 1.

15. N.d., *Ibid.*

16. October 12, 1933, *Ibid.*

17. N.d., HHPL, Poetry sent to HH 1933-64(1).

18. October 25, 1933, FDRL, OF616, Box 1.

19. N.d., HHPL, Poetry sent to HH 1933-64(1).

20. N.d., *Ibid.*

21. January 5, 1936, *Ibid.*

22. N.d., *Ibid.*

23. October 6, 1932, FDRL, DNC, Box 308.

24. N.d., FDRL, OF616, Box 10.

25. N.d., *Ibid.*, Box 9.

26. April 15, 1936, *Ibid.*, Box 10.

27. January 15, 1936, *Ibid.*, Box 9.

28. June 29, 1935, *Ibid.*, Box 5.

29. N.d., *Ibid.*, Box 10.

30. N.d., *Ibid.*, Box 5.

31. February 29, 1936, *Ibid.*, Box 9.

32. N.d., *Ibid.*, Box 8.

33. N.d., HHPL, Poetry sent to HH 1933-64(1).

34. N.d., FDRL, OF616, Box 10.

35. *New York Times*, January 5, 1939.

36. N.d., FDRL, OF104 1933-36 H-J.

37. N.d., FDRL, OF616, Box 10.

38. N.d., *Ibid.*

39. January 8, 1936, *Ibid.*, Box 9.

40. October 18, 1935, *Ibid.*, Box 6.

41. June 22, 1936, *Ibid.*, Box 10.

42. N.d., *Ibid.*, Box 7.

43. N.d., *Ibid.*, Box 2.

44. September 2, 1935, *Ibid.*, Box 6.

45. July 1, 1936, FDRL, OF104, Box 1.

46. N.d., FDRL, OF104, 1939 N-Z.

47. February 23, 1938, *Ibid.*

48. N.d., FDRL, OF616, Box 8.

49. June 26, 1936, *Ibid.*, Box 10.

50. April 15, 1936, *Ibid.*

51. July 29, 1936, *Ibid.*

52. February 8, 1939, *Ibid.*, Box 15.

53. July 1, 1937, FDRL, OF104, 1939 N-Z.

54. *Ibid.*

55. May 5, 1938, FDRL, OF616, Box 14.

56. June 15, 1937, FDRL, OF104, 1939 N-Z.

57. August 22, 1940, FDRL, OF616, Box 17.

58. October 2, 1936, *Ibid.*, Box 11.

59. 1938, FDRL, OF104, Box 2.

60. N.d., FDRL, OF616, Box 3.

61. *Ibid.*

62. December 5, 1935, FDRL, OF616, Box 8.

63. October 13, 1937, *Ibid.*, Box 13.

64. *Ibid.*

65. October 29, 1994, *Ibid.*, Box 3.

66. N.d., *Ibid.*, Box 9.

67. March 4, 1937, FDRL, OF104, 1937-39 I-M.

*Chapter 7*

1. For a study of the sentiment in one state, see Donald W. Whisenhunt, *Texas in the Depression: The Hoover Years* (New York: Garland, 1983), 197-215.

2. *Ibid.*

3. October 16, 1930, HHPL, Poetry 1929-1930.

4. *Ibid.*

5. *Dallas*, 9 (June, 1930), 12.

6. March 14, 1931, HHPL, Poetry 1931.

7. November 10, 1931, HHPL, *Ibid.*

8. Christopher Morley, "What the President Reads," *Saturday Review of Literature*, 9 (September 24, 1932), 117-120.

9. September 30, 1932, HHPL, Poetry 1932, September 30.

10. September 29, 1932, HHPL, Poetry 1932, September 29.

11. September 26, 1932, HHPL, Poetry 1932, September 26.

12. September 25, 1932, HHPL, Poetry 1932, September 16-25.

13. September 23, 1932, HHPL, *Ibid.*

14. *Ibid.*

15. *Monty's Monthly*, November, 1932, 14.

16. May 13, 1932, HHPL, Poetry 1932, May.

17. October 16, 1932, HHPL, Poetry 1932, October 6-10.

18. November 21, 1933, FDRL, OF104, 1933-36 H-J.

19. August 5, 1933, FDRL, OF104, 1933-36, N-P.

20. August 16, 1935, FDRL, OF616, Box 6.

21. January 5, 1935, FDRL, OF616, Box 4.

22. For a discussion of the concept, see William E. Leuchtenburg, *Franklin Roosevelt and the New Deal, 1932-1940* (New York: Harper, 1963), 162-164.

23. December 6, 1937, FDRL, OF104, 1937-39, A-C.

24. *Ibid.*

25. *Ibid.*

26. January 29, 1938, FDRL, OF104, Box 2.

27. September 24, 1932, HHPL, Poetry 1932, September 16-25.

28. December 17, 1932, FDRL, DNC, Box 322.

29. June 19, 1935, FDRL, OF616, Box 5.

30. September 27, 1935, FDRL, OF616, Box 6.

31. January 15, 1936, FDRL, OF616, Box 9.

32. July 6, 1937, FDRL, OF616, Box 13.

33. *Ibid.*

34. September 20, 1939, FDRL, OF616, Box 15.

35. October 21, 1935, FDRL, OF616, Box 6.

36. December 12, 1935, FDRL, OF616, Box 8.

37. October 17, 1935, FDRL, *Ibid.*

38. August 14, 1935, FDRL, OF616, Box 6.

39. June 29, 1935, FDRL, OF616, Box 5.

40. November 20, 1935, FDRL, OF616, Box 7.

41. November 30, 1937, FDRL, OF616, Box 13.

42. April 6, 1939, FDRL, OF616, Box 15.

43. October 6, 1938, FDRL, OF104, 1939 N-Z.

44. October 1, 1939, FDRL, OF104, Box 3.

45. May 1, 1939, FDRL, OF616, Box 15.

46. October 22, 1939, FDRL, OF104, 1937-39 A-C.

47. July 12, 1940, FDRL, OF104, Box 4.

48. 1940, FDRL, *Ibid.*

49. September 9, 1940, FDRL, *Ibid.*

50. April 17, 1939, FDRL, OF616, Box 15.

51. July 8, 1940, FDRL, OF616, Box 17.

52. July 1, 1941, FDRL, OF616, Box 20.

53. May 29, 1941, FDRL, *Ibid.*

54. For a study of one state, see Donald W. Whisenhunt, "The Texan as a Radical," *Social Science Journal*, 14 (October 1977).

55. April 5, 1935, FDRL, OF616, Box 4.

56. January 15, 1936, FDRL, OF616, Box 9.

57. May 15, 1937, FDRL, OF41, Box 28.

58. October 3, 1932, FDRL, DNC, Box 16.
59. July 13, 1932, HHPL, Poetry 1932 June-July.
60. December 31, 1934, FDRL, OF616, Box 4.
61. January 5, 1935, FDRL, *Ibid.*
62. July 28, 1935, FDRL, OF616, Box 6.
63. November 11, 1935, FDRL, OF616, Box 7.
64. August 13, 1936, FDRL, OF616, Box 11.
65. October 10, 1936, FDRL, *Ibid.*
66. July 25, 1938, FDRL, OF616, Box 14.
67. October 16, 1936, FDRL, OF616, Box 11.
68. January 28, 1937, FDRL, OF616, Box 12.
69. October 2, 1935, HHPL, Poetry sent to HH 1933-64 (1).


*Chapter 8*


1. George Wolfskill and John A. Hudson, *All But the People: Franklin D. Roosevelt and His Critics, 1933-39* (New York: Macmillan, 1969).
2. N.d., HHPL, Poetry 1933 & undated.
3. November 1, 1932, HHPL, Poetry 1932, November 1-5.
4. February 5, 1933, HHPL, Poetry 1933 & undated.
5. Booklet, *Roosevelt*, July 12, 1935, FDRL, PPF 200-A, Box 3.
6. N.d., HHPL, Poetry sent to HH 1933-64 (1).
7. N.d., *Ibid.*
8. N.d., *Ibid.*
9. N.d. HHPL, Poetry 1932 October 1-5.
10. N.d., HHPL, Poetry 1932 November 1-5.
11. February 5, 1933, HHPL, Poetry 1933 & undated.
12. February 1, 1993, *Ibid.*
13. N.d., HHPL, Poetry sent to HH 1933-64(1).
14. N.d., *Ibid.*
15. October 2, 1935, *Ibid.*
16. N.d., *Ibid.*
17. N.d., *Ibid.*
18. Booklet, *Frankie in Wonderland*, n.d., FDRL, PPF 200-A, Box 4.
19. N.d., HHPL, Poetry sent to HH 1933-64(1)
20. October 12, 1935, *Ibid.*
21. N.d., FDRL, OF616, Box 11.
22. *Ibid.*
23. N.d., FDRL, OF616, Box 10.
24. N.d., HHPL, Poetry sent to HH 1933-64(1).
25. *Ibid.*

26. N.d., *Ibid.*

27. Booklet, *Roosevelt*, July 12, 1935, FDRL, PPF 200-A, Box 3.

28. *Ibid.*

29. N.d., HHPL, Poetry sent to HH 1933-64(1).

30. N.d., *Ibid.*

31. N.d., *Ibid.*

32. N.d., *Ibid.*

33. December 26, 1939, FDRL, OF616, Box 15.

34. N.d., FDRL, OF616, Box 14.

35. October 25, 1934, *Ibid.*, Box 3.

36. N.d., HHPL, Poetry sent to HH 1933-64(1).

37. December 3, 1938, FDRL, OF616, Box 14.

38. N.d., *Ibid.*

39. N.d., FDRL, PPF 200-A, Box 7.

40. N.d., HHPL, Poetry sent to HH 1933-64(1).

41. N.d., *Ibid.*

42. N.d., HHPL, Poetry sent to HH 1933-64(2).

43. N.d., HHPL, Poetry sent to HH 1933-64(1).

44. N.d., *Ibid.*

45. N.d., *Ibid.*

46. N.d., *Ibid.*

47. N.d., *Ibid.*

48. N.d., *Ibid.*

49. March 27, 1936, FDRL, OF616, Box 9.

50. N.d., HHPL, Poetry sent to HH 1933-64(1).

51. N.d., *Ibid.*

52. N.d. FDRL, OF616, Box 10.

53. July 16, 1937, *Ibid.*, Box 13.

54. August 16, 1937, *Ibid.*

55. August 2, 1935, *Ibid.*, Box 6.

56. May 15, 1937, FDRL, OF41, Box 28.

57. February 27, 1937, *Ibid.*, Box 27.

58. January 8, 1936, FDRL, OF616, Box 9.

59. April 8, 1937, FDRL, OF41, Box 96.

60. December 26, 1939, FDRL, OF616, Box 15.

61. N.d., *Ibid.*, Box 14.

62. N.d., HHPL, Poetry sent to HH 1933-64(1).

63. N.d., *Ibid.*

64. March 29, 1939, FDRL, OF616, Box 15.

65. July 4, 1939, *Ibid.*

66. August 9, 1938, *Ibid.*, Box 14.

67. N.d., *Ibid.*; see also Poem, November 22, 1939, HHPL, Poetry sent to H 1933-63(1).

68. December 3, 1938, FDRL, OF616, Box 14.

69. See for example, January 1, 1939, March 29, 1939, *Ibid.*, Box 15.

70. April 18, 1939, FDRL, OF616, Box 14. See also n.d., *Ibid.*, Box 11; n.d., *Ibid.*, Box 6; n.d., *Ibid.*, PPF 200-A, Box 7.

71. See for example November 21, 1939, and n.d., HHPL, Poetry sent to HH 1933-64(1); Poem October 23, 1934, FDRL, OF616, Box 3; n.d., FDRL, PPF 200-A, Box 7.

72. N.d., HHPL, Poetry sent to HH 1933-64(1).

73. November 22, 1939, *Ibid.*

74. N.d., FDRL, PPF 200-A, Box 4.

75. *Ibid.*

76. November 22, 1939, HHPL, Poetry sent to HH 1933-64 (1).

77. N.d., *Ibid.*

78. *Ibid.*

# Index

**217**

Revolution, possibility of, 135, 160-166
Roosevelt, Eleanor, 79, 83, 168; poems critical of, 179-182
"Roosevelt Family," poems critical of," 179-182"
Roosevelt, Franklin D., 2, 3, 4, 5, 6, 7, 8, 10, 35, 37, 41, 42, 45, 48, 63, 64, 60, 72, 74, 75, 79, 78, 108, 109, 118, 119, 127, 128, 144, 159, 161, 162, 163, 165, 166, 199; evaluated, 79; poems criticizing, 167-198; poems praising, 79-104, 128, 129
Roosevelt Presidential Library, 6
Roosevelt, Theodore, 79
Rosner, David, 5

SEC, 63, 105
Second New Deal, 144
Securities and Exchange Act, 63
Securities and Exchange Commission, see SEC
Sinclair, Upton, 52
"Slaves of the Depression": Workers' Letters About Life on the Job, 5
Smith, Alfred, 19, 22, 29, 68, 80, 101, 171
Smith, Ira, 4
Smoot-Hawley Tariff, 59
Smythe, J. Henry, 101
Social Darwinism, 13
Stalin, Josef, 157, 187
Steinbeck, John, 52

Stock Market Crash, 22, 59
Supreme Court, 132, 167, 187; poems about, 188-193
Supreme Court Packing Plan, poems about, 190-193
Sussmann, Leila, 4

Talmadge, Eugene, 101, 119
Tammany Hall, 20, 21
Tariff, as cause of depression, 59
Tennessee Valley Authority, see TVA
Third Term, poems about, 193-194
Townsend, Francis, 101
Transiency, 50-56; youth in, 54-56
Tugwell, Rexford G., 177
TVA, 114; poems about, 129-133

United States v. Butler, 121
University of Texas at Austin, 4

Valentine Collection, 4
Veterans Bonus March, 66

Wall Street, 161, as cause of depression, 61-62
Wallace, Henry, 118, 119, 177
Washington, George, 31, 88
Whitman, Walt, 5
Wilson, Woodrow, 5, 13, 70, 76, 187
Wolfskill, George, 4, 167
World War I, 148, 149-150
WPA, 102, 133, 179; poems about, 125-129

www.ingramcontent.com/pod-product-compliance
Lightning Source LLC
Chambersburg PA
CBHW031247090426
42742CB00007B/345